TENNESSEE WILLIAMS AND THE SOUTH

Tennessee Williams and the South

By Kenneth Holditch
and Richard Freeman Leavitt

UNIVERSITY PRESS OF MISSISSIPPI   JACKSON

www.upress.state.ms.us

04   03   02   4   3   2   1

Library of Congress Cataloging-in-Publication Data

Holditch, W. Kenneth.

  Tennessee Williams and the South / by Kenneth Holditch and Richard
Freeman Leavitt.

    p. cm.

  ISBN 1-57806-410-4 (alk. paper)

  1. Williams, Tennessee, 1911–1983—Knowledge—Southern States. 2.
Literature and society—Southern States—History—20th century. 3.
Dramatists, American—20th century—Biography. 4. Southern States—In
literature. I. Leavitt, Richard F. II. Title.

  PS3545.I5365 Z69 2002

  812'.54—dc21   2002000631

British Library Cataloging-in-Publication Data available

To the memory of my mother and father, Dora and Sidney;
to my friend Ruth Ford; and to the state of Mississippi,
"that schizophrenic piece of heaven," in the words
of novelist Berry Morgan, from which she, Tennessee,
my parents, Ruth Ford, and I all sprang

—K. H.

CONTENTS

INTRODUCTION: *A More Congenial Climate*

"Southern Comfort! What is that, I wonder."

These memorably ironic words are spoken by Blanche DuBois in *A Streetcar Named Desire* as she searches for something to drink in the kitchen of Stella and Stanley Kowalski, her sister and brother-in-law, in the French Quarter of New Orleans. The words originated, of course, in the mind of the dramatist Tennessee Williams, Blanche's creator, who had good reason to associate comfort and happiness with the South, that region of the country in which he had been born and had spent the first seven years of his life. It was for him that "congenial" habitation to which he would return to spend a large part of his adult life, "my native Southland," as he termed it, that gave him inspiration and much of his best material.

During his childhood, while his father, Cornelius Coffin Williams, traveled around the South selling first men's clothing and later shoes, Thomas Lanier Williams and his sister Rose lived with their mother and maternal grandparents in the Episcopal rectories in Columbus, Mississippi, and then in Clarksdale, the site of the Edenic existence that would haunt his memory and also sustain him

after Tom had been transformed into world-renowned playwright Tennessee Williams. When he was asked to comment on the character Aunt Rose Comfort, the elderly relative in *Baby Doll*, he responded that she was the only one in the play who had "grace and poetry," and added, "I have never written about the South any other way." Her name, "Comfort," seems a wonderful metaphor for his feelings about the region, and it takes on an added irony when one knows that he actually had a relative by that name. In real life Rose Comfort, a contemporary of Tom's sister Rose, was a step-cousin from Tennessee whose father had been the judge in the famous Scopes "monkey trial" in 1925. The quality of grace, that ability of southerners to endure in the face of extreme adversity, entranced him. When asked in the 1970s about the condition of his sister Rose, who already had been long hospitalized, he replied that she was "surviving with grace," which constituted perhaps the highest achievement of which the human being was capable.

When Tom was seven, his father, Cornelius, unexpectedly took a job in the offices of the

International Shoe Company and moved his family from Mississippi to St. Louis. Transported at an early age from a joyous childhood, in which he had been the constant object of doting attention from his mother, his sister, and his grandparents, dropped down in that "cold northern city," as he would term St. Louis in *The Glass Menagerie* and even call "the City of St. Pollution," Tom dreamed of what seemed the Paradise on earth they had left behind. That comfortable world was again made palpable for him by the annual visit of his grandmother, which he saw as "a return of grace from exile in the South."

These expressions of devotion to the South are typical of the playwright. Since the end of the War Between the States many southern writers have engaged in a love-hate relationship with the native region, from which they drew inspiration and subject matter. Some passionately resist the regional label, but two major authors who never denied their southernness were William Faulkner and Tennessee Williams. No writer of this century more than Williams, who was strongly influenced by his Mississippi youth and his many years of residence in New Orleans and Key West, has been as markedly southern in his choice of settings, characters, plots, and themes. Mention of his name evokes for readers and playgoers all over the world a vivid image of the Deep South. No influence, other than his family and his sexual orientation, had as much influence on shaping the dramatist's work as the South that pro-

duced him. Oddly, he generally did not concern himself with the two major historical events of the region, the Civil War and Reconstruction. One of his few references to the war is in the poem "Impressions Through a Pennsy Window" when the persona, reentering the Deep South from the North, briefly and guiltily senses, almost hears, "the dreadful anachronism of The Rebel Yell," an experience that makes him "wonder at blood."

Williams's explanation for his love of the South and his reason for writing much of his best literature about it reveals the depths of his feelings and the extent to which the memory of childhood remained an influence on his life, his consciousness, and his work. Williams commented that although he was disturbed by the ultra-conservative point of view prevalent in the region, it was "out of a regret for a South that no longer exists that I write of the forces that have destroyed it." One is reminded of the beleaguered Blanche DuBois, clinging to her vision, part reality, part illusion, of that *Gone-with-the-Wind* South represented by the plantation Belle Reve, and her confrontation in New Orleans with the "New Man" of the modern age, Stanley Kowalski, who destroys her just as the forces he represents destroyed much of the best of the Old South. Like Faulkner, Tennessee deplored the soulless quality of the so-called "New South," the land of Snopeses and Kowalskis, in which there is no place for a Blanche DuBois who yearns for music and poetry and art. With his heroine Tennessee believed that holding back "with the apes" had become the order of the day.

In a 1970s interview Williams insisted that despite what had been lost, there was still in the South "a greater sense of honor, of decency," as well as "the Cavalier tradition the North never had and less of the dog-eat-dog attitude." On one occasion he remarked, perhaps with just a bit of humorous malice in his tone, that he did not write about the North "because—so far as I know—they never had anything to lose, culturally . . . ," while the South "once had a way of life that I am just old enough to remember," marked by "grace, elegance" and was "not a society based on money as in the North. I write out of regret for that."

He wrote of *Orpheus Descending* that the drama was intended to expose what he felt to be corrupt in the contemporary world, the forces that he believed had destroyed the way of life of the Old South, represented in *A Streetcar Named Desire* by Blanche's "elegance, a love of the beautiful, a romantic attitude toward life." Indeed, he relates his credo to that attitude when he identifies his "main theme" as "a violent protest against those things that defeat it." The South with its "tragic history," Harry Rasky writes, is the perfect setting for the "lonely, trapped, and desperate" characters who populate Tennessee's plays; in other words, locale and the characters' predicaments are intertwined. For romantic writers, Williams among them, the South and its past provided a source of material and

a theatre of the imagination in which to stage it. Indeed, in an age when writers in other parts of the country had chosen ultra-realism as their focus, southern authors continued to write in the romantic mode. In an interview in the *Oxford American* artist Sally Mann compares southern artists to snake-handlers: "What snake venom is to them, romanticism is to the southern artist, a terrible risk, and a ticket to transcendence." Through the half century of Tennessee's career some theatre critics continued to treat him as a realist, when in fact he is much more accurately described as a *romantic,* an *idealist,* an *impressionist.* Repeatedly in his dramas he plays on the dichotomy between the real and the ideal, the physical and the spiritual. It is this painful separation between what she dreams of and her reality that alters Alma Winemiller's life in *Summer and Smoke* and motivates Blanche DuBois to try to "redecorate" the environment of her present circumstances into some semblance of order and beauty. The desperately breathless flow of words from both women reveals, even as it attempts to veil, their entrapment between the idealized past and the all too real present.

It is, of course, the grace and elegance of the Old South for which Amanda Wingfield in *The Glass Menagerie* grieves and yearns, and the description of her in the stage directions makes it clear that we should view her character with sympathy; that however much the character Tom may be at odds with his mother, there is something of Amanda in him as well as in the dramatist. Just as the faded southern belle exists in a kind of metaphorical vacuum between the remembered and the romanticized past on the one hand and a present that is, for her, almost unthinkable, so does the poet-playwright Tennessee Williams dwell between a real, sometimes almost intolerable world and an idealized state of existence akin to that portrayed in one of his favorite poems, the "Ode to a Nightingale" of John Keats. The Old South of Amanda Wingfield's memory is mythic, surely transformed by time into something grander and more idyllic than reality, and her flights of fancy into this dream world parallel the flight of the nightingale which the poet aches to emulate. Similar memories from the playwright's childhood, intensified by the stories his mother told, instilled in him a vision of a prelapsarian Paradise that he glorifies as it is remembered, not perhaps as it actually was. Both he and his characters grieve as they recognize that what has been will be no more.

Tennessee Williams unashamedly acknowledged his tendency "to poeticize," a result of his origins, and offered that trait as the reason for creating "southern heroines" who tend to "gild the lily" and "speak in a rather florid style." He wrote of southern characters, he once remarked, "Because I know and understand their moods and personalities better and because I am both familiar and in complete sympathy with the flavor and mode of their speech." It was not just the flow of that speech that intrigued him, but also its charm: "Southerners express things in a way that is humorous, colorful, graphic." They speak "much more lyrically, especially the women," and even southern politicians, he observed, employ much more florid language than their northern counterparts, with "a very picturesque turn of phrase" and "a sort of rhetoric that I used for Big Daddy in *Cat on a Hot Tin Roof.*" In a discussion with the Japanese novelist Yukio Mishima, Williams asked, "Have you ever known a southerner who wasn't long-winded? I mean, a southerner not afflicted with terminal asthma?"

If we assume Amanda Wingfield in *The Glass Menagerie* to be a fairly accurate portrayal of Edwina Williams, then the author's mother was definitely one of those southern ladies who tend to gild the lily, but he also attributed to his father, a Tennessean by birth, "a great gift for idiom." (The phrase "Cat on a Hot Tin Roof" was a favorite of Cornelius that his son adopted for a title.) Williams was intrigued by an interesting irony in the contrast between the southern woman's charm of demeanor and speech and the fact that she could be firm, decisive, even cruel, a "Steel Magnolia," if you will. (His friends the novelist Carson McCullers of Georgia and the actress Tallulah Bankhead of Alabama exemplified for him that ironic, sometimes incendiary admixture of traits.) Life, he believed, had taught these women to be survivors, a quality that the playwright admired as much as did William Faulkner.

Tennessee once remarked, "So many of these southern ladies that I meet nowadays with these Garden District airs and their plantation niceties of behavior—hah. You find them hard as nails underneath." Certainly that was the case with Violet Venable of *Suddenly Last Summer*, resident of the exclusive Garden District in uptown New Orleans, and the same, he insisted, was also true of Blanche DuBois. When asked about the ultimate fate of Blanche, he always insisted that despite the fact that *Streetcar* ended in her being taken away to a mental institution, she would endure, perhaps even prevail against her adversities.

Because it is the passage of time that destroys that which was—or is remembered as—grand, pure, and innocent, the romantic southerners frequently tend to cling to the past. Certainly this is true of Amanda Wingfield, who in her monologues in *The Glass Menagerie* returns repeatedly to the days and climate of her youth for the consolation and support it takes to endure. She chastises her son as "the only young man that I know of who ignores the fact that the future becomes the present, the present becomes the past, and the past turns into everlasting regret if you don't plan for it"—ironic, since what she is describing is the very pattern of her own life, a fact she later acknowledges to Jim O'Connor, the Gentleman Caller, when she says, "I wasn't pre-pared for what the future brought me." For the southerner, as Gavin Stevens observes in Faulkner's *Requiem for a Nun*, "The past is not dead; it's not even past"—and certainly for the son of Edwina Williams, the same was true. For Tennessee Williams that past was the South of his youth, the strongest and most abiding influence on his creations.

The authors gratefully acknowledge the assistance of the following people:

Charles and Abbe Ayala, Chebie Gaines Bateman, Carl and Dixie Butler, Brenda Caradine, Phil and Hilda Clark, Joseph DeSalvo, Jr., John Donnels, Tom Erhardt, Elaine Evans, Frances Evans, Richard and Kristina Ford, Peggy Fox, Ed Frank, Jack Fricks, Dr. and Mrs. Thomas H. Gandy, David Gooch, Allean Hale, Christopher Harris, Robert Hines, the Historic New Orleans Collection, Catherine Jannik, Don Lee Keith, Susan Knoer, Jordan Massee, Panny Mayfield, Ron and Mimi Miller, Jack Oatman, Dennis Palmore, Earl G. Perry Jr., Sally Polhemus, Harry Rasky, St. Elizabeth's School, Paul St. Martin, JoAnne Sealy, Martha Sparrow, Nancy Tischler, Arthur Tong, Linda White, Dakin and Joyce Williams, Donald Windham, Yvonne Galatoire Winn, and Sarah Wright. Our special thanks to Anne Stascavage, whose astute editing contributed so much to the photo legends in this book.

TENNESSEE WILLIAMS AND THE SOUTH

"Have you ever seen, or looked at a picture, of a Gothic cathedral? . . . How everything reaches up, how everything seems to be straining for something out of the reach of stone — or human — fingers? . . . reaching up to something beyond attainment!"

SUMMER AND SMOKE

Tennessee was baptized at St. Paul's Episcopal Church
in Columbus, Mississippi.

A Dark, Wide World
You Can Breathe In

Thomas Lanier Williams III, destined to be known to the world as "Tennessee," was born on 26 March, 1911, in Columbus, a town in the hills of northeast Mississippi not far from the Alabama line. It was Palm Sunday, and the Reverend Walter Dakin, grandfather of the new baby, was conducting services at St. Paul's Episcopal Church when his daughter went into labor. Edwina Dakin was rushed to a clinic, arriving only minutes before her son was born. A few days later he was christened at St. Paul's and named for his paternal grandfather, Thomas Lanier Williams II, who had died in 1908.

Originally called Possum Town by the local Indians, Columbus was incorporated in 1821 and immediately began to grow. It had become by the mid-nineteenth century a beautiful town, sprawled across the rolling hills between the Tombigbee and the Luxapalila Rivers. Even today, despite the strip malls that spread out like some ugly infection from the center of town, the Columbus of old is still there, seemingly barely touched by time. Along its tree-lined streets are more than two hundred antebellum mansions, set deep in large lots amid oaks, magnolias, and cedars, and every spring the yards and gardens are magically transformed by an astounding abundance of flowers—azaleas, camellias, gardenias, Confederate jasmine, and bridal wreath—and blooming trees—dogwood, redbud, plum, and pear—into a riot of fragrance and color.

Tom was the second child of his parents; his sister Rose had been born in 1909. His mother, Edwina Dakin Williams, had herself been born in Ohio, an ironic detail, consider-

Thomas Lanier Williams III

Given his playwright's concern for religious themes, his birth date was auspicious— 26 March 1911, Palm Sunday.

Rev. Dakin's first appointment in Mississippi
was at the chapel in Church Hill, Mississippi.

Port Gibson Presbyterian Church

"There is the Episcopal church. My father was rector of it before
his death. . . . Instead of a cross on top of the steeple, it has an
enormous gilded hand with its index finger pointing straight up,
accusingly, at—heaven." (*The Eccentricities of a Nightingale*)

ing the fact that by her teen years she had become in her language and lifestyle the quintes-
sential southern belle. She did, however, spend
several of her formative years in Tennessee,
when her father was studying for the ministry
at the University of the South in Sewanee,
Tennessee. Like most other graduates of that
institution—one famous alumnus, William
Alexander Percy, referred to them as "the Arcadians"—Reverend Dakin would forever hold
his alma mater dear to his heart, and the
grandfather's devotion would decades later be
rewarded by the largess of his playwright-
grandson's will.

Even though the family returned to Ohio
after the time in Sewanee, when Edwina was in
her teens, her father subsequently accepted a
series of pulpits in the South, first in Cleve-
land, Tennessee, then at the lovely antebellum

chapel at Church Hill, near Natchez, Mississippi, then in the town of Port Gibson, where
the "southernization" of the young woman
seems to have been completed. It was in Port
Gibson that the playwright's mother insisted
that she had spent the happiest of her youthful
years, and in Tennessee's drama *The Eccentricities of a Nightingale* when Alma Winemiller

Early in the twentieth century, Rev. and Mrs. Dakin lived in Port Gibson, Mississippi, where daughter Edwina's social life flourished. She would later recall it as the happiest time in her life.

"One Sunday in Blue Mountain—your mother received—seventeen!—gentleman callers! Why, sometimes there weren't enough chairs to accommodate them all. . . . It wasn't enough for a girl to be possessed of a pretty face and a graceful figure—although I wasn't slighted in either respect. She also needed to have a nimble wit and tongue to meet all occasions."

THE GLASS MENAGERIE

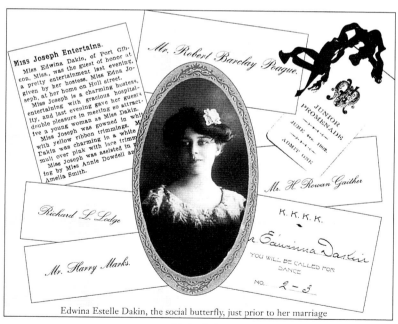

Edwina Estelle Dakin, the social butterfly, just prior to her marriage

Edwina Dakin

Thomas Lanier Williams II

Isabel Coffin Williams,
paternal grandmother

"My father's mother . . .
died at the age of twenty-
eight from tuberculosis.
This meant that my father
grew up mostly without
the emollient influence of a
mother." (*Memoirs*)

"My paternal grandfather . . . practically exhausted
the family fortune, mostly in real estate, by running
repeatedly for Governor against a popular dema-
gogue. . . . Although educated in law at Heidelberg, he
never rose higher in politics than State Railroad
Commissioner. He was a great lady's man—I wonder if
he would have tolerated me." (*Memoirs*)

Tennessee's ancestor cousin
Sidney Lanier. Tennessee could
recite from memory his
favorite lines from Lanier's
"The Marshes of Glynn."

I will fly in the greatness
of God as the marsh-hen flies
In the freedom that fills
at the space twix't the marsh
and the skies. . . .
O, like to the greatness of God
is the greatness within
the range of the marshes,
the liberal marshes of Glynn.

Polly McClung

speaks of the Episcopal Church in Glorious Hill, with its unusual steeple, she is actually describing the Port Gibson Presbyterian Church. It was in 1905 that the Dakins and their daughter moved to Columbus, Mississippi, where they would remain until 1 December 1913. It was in Columbus that Edwina Dakin met Cornelius Williams in 1905 and two years later, 3 June 1907, married him.

Cornelius Coffin Williams was the true southerner of the family, born and reared in Knoxville, Tennessee, the son of Thomas Lanier Williams II, for whom Cornelius's son would be named, and Isabel Coffin Williams. Cornelius was a descendant of several pioneer families of that state and the region—Seviers, Laniers, Calhouns, and Williamses. This lineage seems to have played no small part in Edwina's decision to accept Cornelius's proposal. One of his ancestors was General James White, the founder of Knoxville, whose granddaughter, Polly McClung, was by marriage a great-great-great aunt of Tennessee's. She was "the first American coed," the playwright wrote Donald Windham, when Tennessee was invited to the University of Tennessee in 1945 to unveil a portrait of her on the occasion of the school's naming a hall for her. Two other distinguished members of his family tree were poets Tristram Coffin and Sidney Lanier, a major Confederate author, who wrote not only verse but also a novel, *Tiger Lilies*, based on his experiences as a federal prisoner of war. Through the Williams line

John "Nollichucky Jack" Sevier

"My father's lineage was an illustrious one, now gone a bit to seed, at least in prominence. He was directly descended from the brother Valentine of Tennessee's first Governor John Sevier" (*Memoirs*)

The Old Gray Cemetery in the family seat of Knoxville is the burial site for the many members of the Williams family, the last being the dramatist's father, Cornelius Coffin Williams, in 1957.

Cornelius could claim as ancestors an early senator from the state which in the late 1930s would provide his playwright-son with his famous *nom de plume*. Through the Seviers, who were Huguenots, Cornelius was related to John Sevier, the first governor of Tennessee, and another illustrious ancestor from that branch was a brother of St. Francis Xavier, Valentine Xavier, whose American descendants changed the spelling of the name to "Sevier." Cornelius's family came from Knoxville, and many of the Williamses, including Cornelius himself, are buried in the old Gray Cemetery there.

The genealogy of the playwright's family is intriguing for a number of reasons. Among the strongest elements of the southern psyche are the familial attachment and pride of ancestry, and the close family ties that exist in the South were even stronger when Thomas Lanier Williams was a child. Despite what skeletons may hang in the family closet, there is a sense of security and pride in *belonging*, in being a part of that unit identified by blood ties. Even now in small towns in the South the appearance of a stranger on the scene is likely to evoke from elders the age-old, ubiquitous question, "Who are his people?" Those who have moved to a town within living memory are likely to be referred to as "come-heres."

By 1900 most members of the old "aristocracy" of the South could best be described as "decayed gentry," having lost whatever fortunes they may ever have possessed in a series of regional disasters: the Civil War, Reconstruc-tion, and several devastating depressions. These reverses, however, seem to have intensified in many southerners a love for, even obsession with, the past and their antecedents. Even though he often disavowed and made fun of ancestor worship, Tennessee, like many, certainly including his mother, took a distinct pride in the history of his family. He considered using the name Valentine Xavier as a *nom de plume* before settling on "Tennessee" and did employ that ancestral name for the male protagonist of *Orpheus Descending*. His use of the name Jonathan Coffin for the ancient poet in *The Night of the Iguana* is an allusion to his New England ancestors.

Given the importance of women as companions and influences in Tennessee's later life and as characters in his plays, it is interesting to note the predominance of female relatives on the playwright's paternal side. His grandmother, Isabel Coffin Williams, was a descendant of an important New England family. One of his father's sisters, Ella, was a nurse in World War I, and the other, another Isabel and Tennessee's favorite, was so strong that he could describe her as the only woman who could intimidate his mother, the indomitable Edwina. So forceful was the character of "Aunt Belle" that Tennessee on several occasions attributed the origin of some qualities of Blanche DuBois to her.

From his mother and her parents Tennessee inherited yet another southern trait, a deeply ingrained religious, Puritanical con-

Tennessee's aunt Ella Williams

Uncle Will and Aunt Belle Brownlow

sciousness, later reflected in play after play. One facet of that conviction was the comfort derived from faith, but another darker aspect was the strong Calvinistic bent that has long marked the southern psyche and southern literature. Writers from the region, even those who have abandoned organized religion, more often than not retain their "Christ-haunted" mentality, to which the Calvinistic Catholic author Flannery O'Connor refers. Tennessee frequently commented on that quality in his character, to the amazement of some of his friends, but much of the tension in his works derives from the struggle between his two natures: romantic and Puritan.

During the early years of Tom's life his father was on the road as a traveling salesman, paying only periodic visits to his wife and children as they continued to live with the Dakins in a variety of Episcopal rectories in southern towns. The house in Columbus in which Tom spent his first two years is a two-story Victorian cottage with Gothic trimmings. As the rectory it was located next to the Episcopal church, but in recent years it has been relocated a block away from the church and converted into the Columbus Visitors Center. When Tom was two, Reverend Dakin moved his wife, daughter, and grandchildren to Nashville, where he had accepted a two-year appointment as rector at the Church of the Advent.

It is interesting to speculate what use the future dramatist might have made, had the family remained in Columbus, of the town's

Tennessee's first home was the gothic rectory of St. Paul's Episcopal Church in Columbus, Mississippi. Today, the house is a visitor's center.

magnificent Federalist, Greek Revival, Italianate, Gothic, and Victorian mansions. Indeed, any one of a number of them might well be Belle Reve, the "beautiful dream," lost to Blanche DuBois. Surely it was inevitable that he soaked up some of that atmosphere, and his grandfather, who was apparently something of a gossip, must have relayed tales to young Tom not only about the people of the Delta but also about those in Columbus. One story in the town concerned a woman who had in her possession a letter of Lord Byron's. This became the inspiration for the one-act play "Lord Byron's Love Letter," set in New Orleans, in which an elderly woman has a letter the poet wrote to her after they met on the steps of the Acropolis. The actual document was owned by a Columbus native, Julia Meek Geherty, who died in 1953, leaving a large collection of books and other memorabilia. The real letter, however, was, rather than a profession of love, a denial by Byron that he had written a poem entitled "The Vampire," but the story became the seed that blossomed in the dramatist's imagination into a Gothic tale of thwarted romance.

The first seven years of Tom's life were spent in several locales—Columbus; Nashville,

Tennessee; Canton, Mississippi; and finally Clarksdale, Mississippi, where Reverend and Mrs. Dakin settled with their expanded family in 1915 when the minister was appointed rector of St. George's, a position he would hold longer than any other of his ministerial career. During that period Cornelius Williams seems, like his counterpart in *The Glass Menagerie*, to have fallen in love with long distance, and his absence represented more of a blessing than a deprivation for Edwina and her two children. The marriage had certainly proven to be quite the opposite of what Edwina seems to have expected: her husband, despite his fine southern

Cornelius Coffin Williams

"Often the voice of my father was jovial or boisterous . . . sometimes harsh . . . sometimes it sounded like thunder. He was a big man . . . a benign bigness. You wanted to shrink away from it, to hide yourself." (*Memoirs*)

genealogy, turned out to be a heavy drinker, a gambler, and a womanizer. Both Rose and Tom were terrified of him, and later, after the birth of the third child, Dakin, Cornelius directed whatever love he had to share with his children toward Dakin and, in effect, spurned his first two offspring. One can only speculate as to Cornelius's feelings about his misalliance with Edwina, though it appears likely that in their own ways the two mismatched people loved each other. (Later, after the three children were grown, the couple would separate and the husband would return to Tennessee.) Cornelius's career as a salesman—he sold Red Goose shoes—is reflected in his son's portrayal of Mr. Charlie Colton, "the last of the Delta drummers" in the short play "The Last of My Solid Gold Watches."

The southern idyll ended for Rose and Tom when their father took a job in St. Louis and moved his family from Clarksdale to that "cold northern city" of *The Glass Menagerie* later referred to by Tennessee as "a city I dread." Tennessee described that uprooting to Harry Rasky as a move to the "heartland of America," which he and his sister, he added with characteristic humor, found "rather heartless, you might say." Rasky, who produced a film, *Tennessee Williams's South,* for Canadian television, later wrote a book about his friendship with the playwright, *A Portrait in Laughter and Lamentation,* in which he noted that "for Tennessee, before bewilderment, there was the South of ease and peace." In his *Memoirs* Tennessee wrote of those early years in Mississippi as "the most joyously innocent of my life, due to the beneficent homelife provided by my beloved Dakin grandparents. . . ."

Tennessee returned to Columbus only a couple of times, once in 1951, when he was interviewed by newspaperman Douglas Bateman and accompanied the Reverend Dakin on visits to old friends. Their host during that visit was D. Douglas Patty, who entertained grandfather and grandson lavishly and was apparently enraged when Tennessee did not bother to write a thank-you note for the hospitality.

Many a seven-year-old, moved from one part of the country to another, would soon have adapted to his new home and felt as if he belonged there, but southerners, as noted above, have deep roots in their own native soil and do not tend to forget the land that gave them birth. There is an old saying in Mississippi that if two natives of the state, unknown to each other, are in a room filled with five hundred people anywhere in the world, they will find each other in fifteen minutes; give them half an hour and they will discover that they are cousins.

In St. Louis, Edwina, Tom, and Rose, deprived of the comfort afforded by the Dakins in their southern haven, became to some de-

Tennessee and Douglas Bateman

gree a new family, isolated with the long-absent but suddenly very present Cornelius in an environment they found uncongenial. The result was an intensification of the problems that had always existed among the four of them. In the opening line of *Anna Karenina* Leo Tolstoi writes that "happy families are all alike; every unhappy family is unhappy in its own way," and the misery of the Williams family was in many ways unique. While growing up, Tom endured the quarrels that were an integral part of the disruptive misalliance of his parents, the disdain Cornelius Williams openly displayed for his creative son, and his own private guilt over

Tom, age twelve, in St. Louis

"The malign exercise of snobbery in 'Middle American' life was an utterly new experience to Rose and to me and I think its sudden and harsh discovery had a very traumatic effect on our lives. It had never occurred to us that material disadvantages could cut us off from friends. It was about this time, age eleven or twelve, that I started writing stories." (*Memoirs*)

Of Roses

All roses are enchantment to the wise.
The veil of sophistry drawn from the eyes,
the heart washed clean of an accustomed
stain by gusts of memory as fresh as rain.

In the confines of gardens or grown wild
they are the crystal vision of a child,
unstained by craft, undisciplined by
grief, sweet as child's laughter, and as
wild and brief . . .

AN EARLY POEM BY WILLIAMS

Rose, age seven

the growing mental dysfunction of his beloved sister Rose, a condition which would finally result in her being subjected to a prefrontal lobotomy and later institutionalized in the 1940s. Rose, the prototype of Laura in *The Glass Menagerie*, died in 1996 at eighty-six, having dwelt for half a century in that twilight zone of artificially created innocence that sadly marks the lobotomized, the extended second childhood into which that radical operation had thrust her unawares. She was probably unable, alas, to appreciate the fact that in every one of her brother's plays, her name appears and that there are in all of them repeated references to her in symbolic terms.

Pained beyond measure by these personal agonies, unhappy with the kind of life he found in his own disconsolate age, an age of disbelief and anxiety, Williams set out to create his own new world, to impose an imaginary order upon an all-too-real modern chaos. The further removed he was from his childhood in Mississippi, the more those early years seemed transformed for him into an ideal time, an innocent and painless existence in which contentment was the order of the day. From these memories, acted upon by his subsequent suffering—the unhappy, even perhaps violent, relationship of his parents; his sister's deteriorating mental condition and the agonies she

In *The Night of the Iguana*, the character of Nonno (Alan Webb), the world's oldest living poet was based on grandfather Dakin. Also appearing in this scene are Patrick O'Neal, Margaret Leighton, and Bette Davis.

"O Courage, could you not as well/Select a second place to dwell,/Not only in that golden tree/But in the frightened heart of me?" (*Night of the Iguana*)

endured; the isolation and silence long imposed upon him because of his sexual orientation; and, after years of the success of his dramas, the unexpected animosity and derision of critics late in his career—from all those adversities, he certainly made sweet uses, in Shakespeare's metaphor, in creating his art.

Williams drew his material from all members of his extended family. His grandfather Dakin became Nonno, the "oldest living, practicing poet" in *The Night of the Iguana,* just as Reverend Dakin was the "oldest living graduate of Sewanee" for a number of his last years. (Williams would leave the mass of his estate in a trust for his sister, but following her death it was to go to Sewanee to commemorate Reverend Dakin.) His grandmother, Rosina Otte Dakin, appears in her real-life role as music teacher in the short story "The Resemblance Between a Violin Case and a Coffin" and as an apparition in "Angel in the Alcove," and the short story "Grand" is a poignant prose portrait of the woman who helped sustain Tennessee in his early writing career. Cornelius, the playwright's father, furnished inspiration for the characters Boss Finley in *Sweet Bird of Youth* and Mr. Charlie Colton in "The Last of My Solid Gold Watches," and some elements of his personality and speech appear in the portrayal of Big Daddy in *Cat on a Hot Tin Roof.* The essay-story "The Man in the Overstuffed Chair" exposes in poignant detail the love-hate

Perhaps no school in America has more faithful alumni than the Arcadians of the University of the South in Sewanee, Tennessee. Williams left a large endowment in memory of his grandfather and today a handsome theatre complex honors his own memory on this gorgeous campus in the Cumberland mountains.

Grandmother Rosina Dakin

"All that is not the worst of me surely comes from Grand, except my Williams anger and endurance, if these be virtues. Whatever I have of gentleness in my nature, and I do have much in response to gentle treatment, comes from the heart of Grand, as does the ineluctable grace and purity of heart that belongs to the other Rose in my life, my sister."
(Memoirs)

Grandfather Dakin

Boss Finley, portrayed by Ed Begley in the movie *Sweet Bird of Youth,* delivers a racist speech.

"I got a mission that I hold sacred to perform in the Southland. . . . When I was fifteen I came down bare-footed out of the red clay hills. . . . Why? Because the Voice of God called me to execute this mission. . . . And what is this mission? I have told you before but I will tell you again. To shield from pollution a blood that I think is not only sacred to me, but sacred to Him."

relationship between Tom and Cornelius Williams and the peace the author achieved with the ghost of the man after his father's death. The mother, of course, inspired the character of Amanda Wingfield in *The Glass Menagerie*—an association Miss Edwina went to her grave denying. Other elements of her character and personal history are reflected in *Summer and Smoke* and various short stories and one-act plays. His sister Rose's presence is felt in all Tennessee's plays, even when she is not embodied within a particular character, as she is in "Portrait of a Madonna," *The Glass Menagerie, Suddenly Last Summer,* and *The Two-Character Play.* In addition, the interaction within the family group to some extent furnishes the paradigm for almost all of the major plays Tennessee created. Their sad but dramatic lives, cast in his memory against the backdrop of a South romanticized by the passage of time and memory, became the material of great drama.

Tennessee Williams's life and works exemplify dramatically Fyodor Dostoyevski's belief that "suffering is the origin of consciousness." (The mention of two Russian authors in relation to Williams is not as strange as it might seem: his favorite writer, and the one he termed his strongest influence, was Anton Chekhov; and his settings, characters, and actions reflect the concerns of Russian writers for the psychological interactions of characters in isolated and defeated societies.) Despite the suffering, for Williams, always in the back of his memory, offering a sanctuary to which he could retreat from whatever "slings and arrows of outrageous fortune" might assail him, was the glorified image of the Mississippi that had shaped him. Idealized though it is, however, it is important to recognize that he was aware of and unflinchingly portrayed the South's flaws, like Faulkner, loving it even as he hated it. There is, for example, the intolerance of the small town in *Battle of Angels* and *Orpheus Descending*, the demagoguery and bigotry of Boss Finley in *Sweet Bird of Youth*, and another unfortunate southern trait, the violence that is in evidence in most of the dramas. Apparently even

his immediate family was not free of such violence.

In a 1969 interview with Jim Seay novelist Jesse Hill Ford, commenting on differences between natives of various Deep South states, stated that Tennesseans tend to brood and Alabamians like to travel and are gregarious. Mississippians he characterized as "hot house plants. They need a certain soil and climate found only in darkest Mississippi or they perish or go mad or drink too much." In a similar vein Tennessee Williams once described Mississippi as "a dark, wide world that you can breathe in." It was a world, as his memory of it indicates, to which he continued to feel drawn. He set plays not only in the Mississippi Delta but on the Gulf Coast: *Sweet Bird of Youth* is set in a beach hotel very similar to the old Buena

The famous old Buena Vista Hotel on the Gulf Coast in Biloxi is surely the inspiration for the Royal Palms Hotel in *Sweet Bird of Youth.*

"I think of it as resembling one of those 'Grand Hotels' around Sorrento or Monte Carlo, set in a palm garden. The style is vaguely 'Moorish.'" (Production Notes, *Sweet Bird of Youth*)

According to the production notes *The Rose Tattoo* was set in
"a village populated mostly by Sicilians somewhere along the
Gulf Coast between New Orleans and Mobile." Actors in this
scene from the original Broadway production include Sal Mineo,
Eli Wallach, and Maureen Stapleton.

"There is something wild in the air, no wind but everything's
moving. . . . Nothing is moving so you can see it moving,
but everything is moving, and I can hear the star-noises."
(*The Rose Tattoo*)

Vista in Biloxi, which was for many years a vacation spot for Mississippians and other southerners. *The Rose Tattoo* is set in an Italian-Sicilian community on the Gulf Coast, and its references to the banana import business and nearby New Orleans clearly locate it on the western Mississippi coast.

Tennessee Williams was fond of quoting one of his collateral ancestors, John Sharp Williams, a Delta planter and distinguished senator from Mississippi in the early twentieth century, who, upon the occasion of his leaving Washington for the last time to return to his beloved home state, asserted that "I'd rather be a hound dog and bay at the moon from my Mississippi plantation than remain in the United States Senate." That persistent southern devotion to the place of one's origin is equally apparent in the attitudes and work of the playwright. As soon as he was free to do so, having finished college and set his mind on a career as a writer, he returned to the South, choosing not the small towns of his native state but the city of New Orleans. Cokie Roberts, the television commentator and author, observed in 1997, "We southerners have a sense of place, and a sense of place gives you a sense of self." Play after play by Williams reflects that association between the human being and place of origin.

Two episodes demonstrate that enduring bond between the dramatist and his native state. In 1941, when, with the help of his new agent Audrey Wood, his play *Battle of Angels*

Mississippi U.S. Senator John Sharp Williams, Tennessee's great uncle

seemed to be Broadway-bound, he expressed his appreciation to her by writing, "When anyone's real nice in Mississippi they are described as precious and that's what you are." Over thirty years later, in the 1970s, Richard Leavitt accompanied Tennessee to a benefit performance of one of his plays on Broadway. Before the curtain rose Tennessee had become so nervous and apprehensive that he insisted they forego the play and retire to a nearby bar. A couple of drinks later Leavitt convinced Tennessee to return to check out the quality of the performance, but in the lobby they were confronted by a theatre official, who refused to let them enter, since seating was restricted to invited guests. "Where are you from?" he demanded, and Tennessee replied, without a beat, "I come from Mississippi." So prevalent and tightly bound was the playwright by those ties to the South of his origin that more than fifty years after he had last spent any time in his native state, he still identified with it. Although he chose for his *nom de plume* the name of the state in which many of his ancestors, illustrious and otherwise, had lived, it was Mississippi that he held close to his heart.

With nursemaid Ozzie, Tom and Rose in "gloriously happy" days

"Do you wish that things could be straight and simple again as they were in your childhood?"

CAMINO REAL

Where You Hang Your Childhood

"Home," Tennessee Williams once wrote, "is where you hang your childhood," and for him Clarksdale, in the heart of the Mississippi Delta, was the one spot on earth where the memories of his early years were stored away until the end of his mortal days. Although he was born in Columbus, the most formative years seem to have been those few that he spent in Clarksdale, 1915-1918, during the First World War. The elegant mansion Belle Reve that Blanche DuBois mourns perhaps reflects Columbus much more than the Delta, although the Cutrer mansion in Clarksdale represented for young Tom the elegance of southern opulence. It was in Clarksdale that the boy Tom acquired many of the stories, characters, names, and locales that were to serve the grown-up author well. In her autobiography, *Remember Me to Tom*, Edwina Williams writes of finding, long after her son had left home, a scrap of paper on which he described his youth in Mississippi, specifically the town of Clarksdale: "Before I was eight, my life was completely unshadowed by fear. . . . My sister and I were gloriously happy. We sailed paper boats in washtubs in water, cut lovely paper dolls out of huge mail-order catalogs, kept two white rabbits under the back porch, baked mud pies in the sun under the front walk, climbed up and down the big wood pile, collected from neighborhood alleys and trash piles bits of colored glass that were diamonds and rubies and sapphires and emeralds." Although he was to spend only one more year in Clarksdale and return on a few occasions after the family's fateful move to St. Louis, the town in which he had spent those crucial years of his childhood continued to affect his imagination and consequently his work. Interestingly, despite the fact that his early life there occurred during the First World War, this historic event seems to have made little impression on his memories.

The strong influence of the Delta on the consciousness of the boy and later the art of the dramatist is understandable if one knows

Edwina reads to Tom and Rose.

the Delta, for its atmosphere is heady and powerful. In *Orpheus Descending* Carol Cutrere, the wayward social-protesting daughter of a Delta planter's family, makes much of the setting when she speaks, almost chants, about there being "something wild in the country," referring to some mystical but natural force not to be contained by human control. Many writers, as well as the inarticulate observers, have been overwhelmed by the powerful aura of what James C. Cobb terms "the most southern place on earth." From that flat, awe-inspiring land-

scape, distinguished by a peculiar mixture of opposing forces and influences and ideas, Tennessee Williams derived much of the inspiration and material for his plays, including, certainly, the steamy sexuality. John Barry notes in *Rising Tide*, his history of the famous 1927 flood, that "in the sultriness of the Delta, sex represented everything." All of Tennessee's plays set in the Delta—*Battle of Angels*, *Orpheus Descending*, *Cat on a Hot Tin Roof*, and *Kingdom of Earth* (*The Seven Descents of Myrtle*), and several one-acts—exemplify this libidinous force of the heady environment and its effect on characters. The lustiness of Maggie in *Cat on a Hot Tin Roof* and the peculiar sexual triangle between two half brothers and the title character in *Kingdom of Earth* (*The Seven Descents of Myrtle*) dramatize that sensuality that Tennessee seems to have associated with the fecundity of the Delta soil. His portrayal of sexuality shocked some audiences but probably would not have surprised many southerners.

The Mississippi Delta has been variously described in history books, atlases, novels, plays, and poems. Novelist Richard Ford refers to it as "the most distilled southern place" and "the South's South," where the "irrepressibly wonderful" landscape is the interesting part. Deltans, according to Ford, tend to be "self-regarding," acutely aware of where they live and possessed of a high regard for their culture, "but in fact," he adds, "the landscape is the interesting part." An oft-repeated metaphorical description of the Delta is David L. Cohn's

Production still, *Cat on a Hot Tin Roof,* with Elizabeth Taylor as Maggie the Cat and Paul Newman as Brick

"You were a wonderful lover. . . . Such a wonderful person to go to bed with, and I think mostly because you were really indifferent to it. Isn't that right? Never had any anxiety about it, did it natural-ly, easily, slowly, with absolute confidence and perfect calm, more like opening a door for a lady or seating her at a table than giving expression to any longing for her."
(Cat on a Hot Tin Roof)

The Peabody Hotel in Memphis at the northern end of the Delta is a site inter-twined with the history of the "Deep South." This photograph, c. 1948, shows the lobby as Tom the boy and Tennessee the young man would have known it.

Catfish Row in Vicksburg is the metaphorical southern terminus of the Mississippi Delta. Vicksburg holds a special place in the southern psyche because its fall on 4 July 1863—one day after the end of the battle of Gettysburg—was the blow that broke the back of the Confederacy.

statement that it originates in the lobby of the Peabody Hotel in Memphis and ends on Catfish Row in Vicksburg. Writer after writer has commented on the Delta's immeasurable dimensions, including Rheta Grimsley Johnson, who sees it as the final haven of "the mythical South." Tennessee referred to it as "this extraordinary country" and "the mysterious landscape" and asserted that it provided him not only with a setting but "with characters of phantom dimensions."

Geographically a flat strip of crescent-shaped land, the Delta stretches from just below Memphis, Tennessee, to Yazoo City, Mississippi. In the poem "The Couple" Tennessee writes, "It's all so wide in the Delta, and so level! / The seasons could walk across it four abreast!" What first strikes a visitor to the region, as Tennessee's lines indicate, is the flatness of the land, level as far as the eye can see, "so primary," Richard Ford says, "that you either love it on first sight or else you feel totally enervated by it."

In the *Pharos* edition of *Battle of Angels* Tennessee records the visit that he and director Margaret Webster made to the Delta in 1940 during preparations for the staging of *Battle*: "We spent two days down there, introducing Peggy to the South—visiting country stores and talking to Delta people. Peggy absorbed the South in twenty-four hours. It was a bit too much for her. She began to look a little punch drunk, seeing just enough of this extraordinary country and its people to make them more

mysterious than they were before." Webster was not the first—or last—to be overwhelmed by a remarkable landscape that envelopes the senses and consciousness of the viewer.

The Delta is, of course, the "Big Woods," the Wilderness, immortalized by Faulkner, but long-gone are the bears, wildcats, and wild boars; gone also are the thousands of acres of giant trees and other heavy vegetation, cut down in the nineteenth century to make way for row crops. The ultra-fertile soil, enriched by centuries of alluvial deposits piled up by the Mississippi and Yazoo Rivers, is fecund and perfect for growing cotton. (So abundant were the crops in the years after the Civil War that sharecropping originated in Mississippi to meet the demand for a large labor force; now, of course, most of the cotton is harvested by machines, while the descendants of sharecroppers work in casinos along the river.) The Mississippi and the Yazoo form the Delta's western boundary, while the demarcation of its eastern boundary is the high ground to the east called the Choctaw Ridge. Driving across the Delta, west to east, one is always startled by the abrupt rise from the low and level Delta into those towering, almost intimidating bluffs.

When Gerald O'Hara instructs his daughter Scarlett in *Gone with the Wind* that "the land, the good rich earth of Tara" is all that matters, he is voicing a long-standing southern tenet of the value of property. In *Cat on a Hot Tin Roof* Big Daddy, described in the stage directions as "the Delta's biggest cotton-planter," boasts that the Delta is "the richest land this side of the Valley Nile," of which he is proud to be the owner of twenty-eight thousand acres. While staying with the Dakins in Memphis in the summer of 1935, Tennessee first read the plays of

A Mississippi Delta scene at cotton harvest time

"I've always sort of admired him in spite of his coarseness, his four-letter words and so forth. Because Big Daddy is what he is, and he makes no bones about it. He hasn't turned gentleman farmer, he's still a Mississippi redneck."
(*Cat on a Hot Tin Roof*)

Anton Chekhov in the library of the nearby liberal arts college, Southwestern at Memphis, and it was during this visit that his play "Cairo, Shanghai, Bombay" was performed in a neighbor's backyard. Tom also recorded that he was delighted by the opportunity to visit the ten-thousand-acre G. D. Perry plantation near Tunica, Mississippi, and "study the life" there. Frances Evans recalls that later, in the 1950s, when Tennessee was visiting Columbus, Mississippi, with his grandfather, he was invited to a party at a plantation in Shuqualak, Mississippi, during which he spent most of the evening asking the men at the party questions about their plantations, particularly how many acres each of them had under cultivation. Mrs. Evans's father-in-law informed Tennessee that his plantation included twenty-eight thousand acres. "Imagine my surprise," she said, "when I saw *Cat on a Hot Tin Roof* and heard Big Daddy describe his plantation in the same way." The character of Big Daddy was drawn from several sources: certainly some of his qualities reflect Cornelius Williams, and the name and to some extent the personality reflect that of the father of Tennessee's friend Jordan Massee, Jr., who was a cousin of novelist Carson McCullers. In 1941 Tennessee visited the Massee home in Georgia and met Jordan Massee, Sr., an enormous man whom his family called "Big Daddy." He was a plantation owner who wore white suits and, according to Lyle

Jordan Massee and son. In 1961 Tennessee inscribed a copy of *Cat on a Hot Tin Roof* to Mr. Jordan Massee, Sr., "To Big Daddy Massee with my affection and esteem."

"But he's a singer," Tennessee responded when Elia Kazan proposed Burl Ives for the role of "Big Daddy" in *Cat on a Hot Tin Roof*. Ives's wonderful performance changed the playwright's mind, and reflected Tennessee's memories of his own father and Mr. Jordan Massee, Sr., of Georgia.

Leverich, boasted about owning "the richest land this side of the Nile."

A major part of the southern umbilical attachment to land involves not merely inhabiting but owning the old homestead. Big Daddy not only took pride in the fact that he possessed all that rich dirt, but he wanted to be sure that it be passed on to the next generation of Pollitts—and the next—and not fall into the wrong hands. An interesting personal anecdote indicates that Tennessee shared that southern obsession with the importance of property. It was 1978; he was in New Orleans for a public reading of his works, and as I walked with him and Don Lee Keith from a restaurant to the auditorium for a rehearsal, Tennessee inquired about the value of property in the French Quarter. When I told him that real estate prices had risen substantially in the past year, he replied, with a chuckle, "Good! You know, I'm just like a sly old fox. I've bought property wherever I went."

One significant element of the Delta is the fact that it is something of an island, separated from the rest of Mississippi and the South not only by its strange topography but also by the insular and often superior attitude of the residents, so much so that David L. Cohn once described it as "a strange and detached fragment thrown off by the whirling comet that is America." Even now Mississippians from the hill country or the prairie land to the east or the Gulf Coast to the south speak of going "*into* the Delta," suggesting, James C. Cobb says, that they are traveling not only in *space* but also in *time* to what is essentially another world. When Tom Williams was living there, despite the existing levee system, inundation was always a threat, as it is in *Battle of Angels*. Tom spent the 1920 and 1921 school year in Clarksdale and the next year a major flood threatened the Delta. When he was sixteen and living in St. Louis, he surely would have heard of the famous 1927 flood from his grandparents as well as from the widespread newspaper reports. As children Tom and Rose would have been required to take quinine tablets every day in the spring and summer as a protection against malaria. This fact of their lives later figures in Amanda's memories in *The Glass Menagerie* when she recalls the summer of jonquils and malaria fever in which she met her future hus-

band. So southern a place was the Delta up until recent years that I recall as a child, living near Clarksdale in the early 1940s, taking those quinine tablets and marching in a Confederate Memorial Day Parade, which included numerous aged veterans of "the War of Northern Aggression" as the bands played "Dixie" and "The Bonnie Blue Flag." Surely Tennessee and his sister must have had similar experiences more than two decades earlier.

The Delta population is a diverse one, including descendants of British settlers of North and South Carolina and Virginia, whose sons and grandsons migrated further south in search of good land and fortune; a large number of blacks, descendants of pre–Civil War slaves; and a surprisingly large percentage of Greeks, Lebanese, Italians, and Chinese. The result is an interesting mélange, one outgrowth of which is a multicultural food, quite different from that in other parts of Mississippi. Delta cuisine includes such regional staples as cornbread and biscuits, fried chicken, country ham, southern barbecued pork, mustard and turnip greens, and other vegetables, all cooked in bacon fat, as well as food for more exotic tastes: stuffed grape and cabbage leaves, kibbe, tabbouleh, spanikopitos, tamales, and, along with the typical heavy southern desserts, including pies and cakes and buttery custards, such foreign specialties as Greek baklava. That ethnic diversity is evident in such Williams works as *Orpheus Descending* and *Baby Doll*.

The ready acceptance of the Dakins in the

St. George's Episcopal
Church, Clarksdale

Delta, which often did not take to outsiders, surely resulted from the grandfather's profession, for the position of Episcopal rector was a respected one in southern towns, and the gentleness of both grandparents endeared them to the parishioners and other residents, who as late as the 1990s remembered them with affection. In a 1932 letter to his mother Tom praises a prayer that his grandfather wrote to commemorate the bicentennial of the birth of George Washington which was printed in the Clarksdale *Daily Register*; he informs his mother that he is happy that his grandfather's "fine qualities are so well appreciated in Clarksdale." While the Reverend Dakin was rector at St. George's Episcopal Church, the family, three generations, lived in the two-story rectory next door. The rector ministered to his congregation and his wife Rose taught violin and piano to local young people. Thus their daughter Edwina moved into the highest level of society, such as it was, and was ready to receive all those "gentlemen callers." She adapted with amazing alacrity to the life of the pretty and popular southern belle, developing all the traits, good and bad, one associates with the type.

The Delta of Mississippi serves as the setting for several of Tennessee Williams's works. There are the full-length dramas—*Spring Storm, Battle of Angels, The Eccentricities of a Nightingale, Summer and Smoke, Cat on a Hot Tin Roof, Orpheus Descending, Kingdom of Earth* (also called *The Seven Descents of Myrtle*), and *Tiger Tail*; the one-act plays—"27 Wagons Full of

Cotton," "The Last of My Solid Gold Watches," "The Unsatisfactory Supper," and "This Property Is Condemned"; and the screenplay *Baby Doll.* There are also short stories—"Something about Him," "Twenty-seven Wagons Full of Cotton," "The Resemblance between a Violin Case and a Coffin," "Three Players of a Summer Game," "The Kingdom of Earth," "Miss Coynte of Greene," and "Completed"; and such poems as "The Couple," "In Jack-O'-Lantern's Weather," and "Recuerdo." In addition, the collection of lyrics collectively called "Blue Mountain Ballads," set to music by Paul Bowles and including "Heavenly Grass," "Lonesome Man," "Cabin," and "Sugar in the Cane," clearly are influenced by the blues singers young Tom Williams heard as a child in the Delta, where that unique musical form was born and is ubiquitous even today. The impressionable young Tom could hardly have missed hearing its rhythms and its words, registering them, and storing them up for later use. Val Xavier in *Orpheus Descending* plays "Heavenly Grass," a blues song with words by Tennessee, on his guitar, which is autographed by blues immortals Bessie Smith and Huddie Ledbetter, known as "Leadbelly." Bessie Smith died in a hospital in Clarksdale in 1937, "murdered," Val says, by "John Barleycorn and Jim Crow." (It is intriguing to think what might have happened had Tennessee's idea of having Val played by Elvis Presley—a fellow Mississippian from Tupelo in the northeastern hill section of the state, a town which is mentioned in several

Bessie Smith, "The Empress of the Blues" and a native of Clarksdale, died there in an automobile accident.

"The name Bessie Smith is written in the stars!—Jim Crow killed Bessie Smith but that's another story. . . . "(*Orpheus Descending*)

Williams plays, including *Battle of Angels*—become a reality. The playwright finally fulfilled his dream of meeting the singer in 1962 when both were in Hollywood.)

Other local details that appear in the dramas and stories include the newspaper the *Clarksdale Register*, the movie house called the Delta Brilliant, and the Alcazar Hotel. In the Delta, since Mississippi had no cities then, Memphis, Tennessee, loomed as a very large presence, and Williams characters frequently

Tennessee Williams met Elvis Presley in Hollywood in 1962. Laurence Harvey stands next to Hal Wallis, the producer. Tennessee thought highly of Presley as an actor and would have loved for him to have played Val in *Orpheus Descending*.

"He is a young man, about 30, who has a kind of wild beauty about him. . . . His remarkable garment is a snakeskin jacket, mottled white, black and gray. He carries a guitar which is covered with inscriptions." (Production note, *Orpheus Decending*)

Production still, *Orpheus Descending,* with Maureen Stapleton, Cliff Robertson, Crahan Denton

Memphis once boasted a popular hotel,
The King Cotton, which Tennessee referred to as The Kotton King
Hotel in his film, *Baby Doll*.

Gayoso Hotel, Memphis

mention two newspapers circulated there, *The Commercial Appeal*, which is still being published, and the now defunct *Press-Scimitar*. There are also numerous references to Memphis hotels, the Peabody, the King Cotton, and the Gayoso, in the last of which his grandfather often resided for long periods late in his life. Baby Doll Meighan in the movie *Baby Doll* and the play *Tiger Tail* threatens to move to the "Kotton King hotel" to escape her husband's sexual advances, and Maggie in *Cat on a Hot Tin Roof* recalls for Brick a Cotton Carnival parade in which a drunk man leaning out a window of the Gayoso spat tobacco juice in the face of the Carnival queen. In 1935 Tom would spend the summer with the Dakins in Memphis, of which he would say on his departure that he did not believe he would "ever become so attached to any other city," a reaction probably partially related to his delight in being away

King and Queen of Cotton

"As for Mae having been a cotton carnival queen . . . well, that's one honor that I don't envy her for! Sit on a brass throne on a tacky float an' ride down Main Street, smilin', and blowin' kisses to all the trash on the street— ."
(*Cat on a Hot Tin Roof*)

from "the City of St. Pollution" and the oppressive presence of his father.

It was during that 1935 visit that Tennessee visited Oxford, Mississippi, seventy-five miles to the southeast of the city, and saw Rowan Oak, the home of William Faulkner, of whom he observed at the time that despite the novelist's reputation in his home town, he was not "stuck-up," but rather, "just absent-minded, like me and other great writers." After he became an established dramatist, he acknowledged the affinity between his work and that of Faulkner and praised the novelist as honest

and "a southern gentleman." In later years he often accompanied his grandfather to Memphis to visit friends and would write two plays with Memphis connections: *Period of Adjustment*, which is set in the city, and *Will Mr. Meriwether Return to Memphis?* one of the late dramas.

Clarksdale's presence is felt as well in other of his plays that are set elsewhere, including *The Glass Menagerie*, in which Amanda recalls her life in Blue Mountain. There are, of course, no mountains or even hills in the Delta, but the town Amanda describes is clearly

Tom, at his grandparents' home in Memphis.

"Why do I resist writing about my plays? The truth is that my plays have been the most important element of my life for God knows how many years. But I feel the plays speak for themselves. And that my life hasn't and that it has been remarkable enough, in its continual contest with madness, to be worth setting upon paper. And my habits of work are so much more private than my daily and nightly existence." (*Memoirs*)

The Cutrer mansion in Clarksdale, home of Mrs. Blanche Cutrer, the daughter of Clarksdale's founder, John Clark

Clarksdale, since she refers to Moon Lake and other sites in the vicinity. In *A Streetcar Named Desire*, although Blanche DuBois is from Laurel, Mississippi, her memories of Belle Reve and her earlier life there and her references to such sites as Moon Lake obviously reflect the Delta. (The use of the names Blue Mountain and Laurel result, no doubt, from the playwright's love of lyrical language and classical allusion.) The Cutrer mansion in downtown Clarksdale, which to a young boy, living with four other people in the limited space of the

As time passed, the Cutrer mansion was purchased by the Catholic Church and became St. Elizabeth's School for Girls. The young maidens dancing here are reminiscent of the gala lawn parties held in the grander days of the Past.

rectory at St. George's Church, must have seemed particularly grand, serves as a major setting for the play *Spring Storm*, written in 1937 but not performed and published until 1999. In several dramas there are references to Two Rivers County, and Clarksdale, like Columbus, is situated between two streams. (When in the 1960s the dramatist set up a management company on the occasion of his buying a townhouse in the French Quarter of New Orleans, he and his realtor, Robert Hines, whimsically named it "Two Rivers Corporation.")

From 1913 to 1918 Tom accompanied his grandfather when the minister made calls on his parishioners throughout Coahoma and neighboring counties. The child must have been intrigued by the Delta landowners and their plantations—most of them not large manor houses like those of Natchez or along the River Road of Louisiana, but practical dwellings on large expanses of rich dark land that had made their owners wealthy. "I always thought of Tom as a small pitcher with big ears," Miss Edwina wrote. "He would sit perfectly quiet never saying a word, listening with every sinew. I don't imagine he missed a trick on these calls." In his preface to *Battle of Angels*, published in *Pharos* in 1945, he recalled those visits in romantic—and very southern—terms: "It seems to me those afternoons were always spent in tremendously tall interiors to which memory gives a Gothic architecture, and that the light was always rather dustily golden."

Tom, age five

"This move [to St. Louis] was preceded, for me, by an illness diagnosed by a small Mississippi town doctor as diphtheria with complications. It lasted a year, was nearly fatal, and changed my nature . . . during this period of illness and solitary games, my mother's overly solicitous attention planted in me the makings of a sissy, much to my father's discontent. I was becoming a decided hybrid, different from the family line of frontiersmen—heroes of east Tennessee." (*Memoirs*)

Tom absorbed into his memory the many sights, smells, and sounds that make up the Delta: blues musicians, mercantile stores, cotton gins, the flat rich fields that stretched for miles, barren in winter, but in the spring, and later, green with cotton plants that in the autumn exploded into white with what an earlier southern poet, Henry Timrod, termed in

King Cotton, in the words of the southern poet Henry Timrod, "the white snow of Southern summers"

Cotton gins in Clarksdale

"Mr. Vacarro—I want you to meet Mrs. Meigham. Baby, this is a very down-at-the-mouth young fellow I want you to cheer up fo' me. He thinks he's out of luck because his cotton gin burnt down. He's got twenty-seven wagons full of cotton to be ginned out on a hurry-up order from his most impo'tant customers in Mobile. ("27 Wagons Full of Cotton")

"Ethnogenesis" "the snows of southern summers" and which Williams described in the
poem "Couples" as "volcanic" and "a noiseless
dynamite. . . ." In three of his plays cotton gins
play a significant part. Late in the fall, as the
gins operate, the Delta air is heavily redolent of
cottonseed oil, a rich buttery aroma that is inescapable but pleasant. There were, as well,
other objects and events that were to haunt
Tom's memory and to help to shape his creations, including the glass menagerie in the
front window of one house and the angel in
the Grange Cemetery, which figures significantly in the drama *Summer and Smoke.*

Southerners are talkers and storytellers, and
among the tales young Tom heard or had repeated to him by his grandfather and stored
up for future use during those few years in the
Delta was that of a drowning at Moon Lake,
one about a man's suicide on the lake shore,
and a story of two men who had shot it out in
the same location. From Clarksdale and vicinity he acquired many of the place names that
recur in his writing: Moon Lake and the casino
there, the Sunflower River, Lyon and the fever
clinic, Friar's Point, Tiger Bayou, and, of
course, the Mississippi River, which in *Battle of
Angels* is threatening to flood and in *The Kingdom of Earth* has already done so.

It was surely during these Delta years young
Tom heard the stories of "the hellfire and
brimstone" preachers who differed markedly
from the refined and ritualized Anglicanism of
the Reverend Dakin and his parishioners. One

An observant Tom Williams would have known this
statue from his boyhood playdays near the Grange
Cemetery in Clarksdale, and his alert mind would have
made a connection between angel and eternity.

"Do you know the name of the angel? . . . You have to read
it with your fingers. I did and it gave me cold shivers. . . . It's
something that goes on and on when life and death and time
and everything else is all through with."
(Summer and Smoke)

Movie still from *Summer and Smoke,* with Geraldine Page and Laurence Harvey

"I will go in a minute, but first I want you to put your hands on my face. . . . Eternity and Miss Alma have such cool hands." (*Summer and Smoke*)

charming event Tom's mother remembered from her son's early years was his digging a large hole in the backyard to "try to find the Debbil." In *The Glass Menagerie* there is a reference to Gypsy Jones, based on the real-life English evangelist Gypsy Smith who preached destruction for sinners throughout the South when the playwright was a boy. Amanda recalls that Gypsy Jones had proclaimed that the Church of the Heavenly Rest in Blue Mountain, Mississippi, had burned down because the Episcopalians were card players. In the short story "The Kingdom of Earth" Chicken relates the story of his having heard Gypsy Smith preach and deciding to give up sex—for a while. In *Cat on a Hot Tin Roof*, after Reverend Tooker remarks that a lot of money was put in the collection plate the past Sunday, Gooper replies, "Reven', you must of been preachin' hell's fire last Sunday!" and in *The Night of the Iguana* a defrocked Episcopal priest, Lawrence Shannon, yearns to return to his pulpit "and preach the gospel of God as Lightning and Thunder."

Through his grandfather young Tom met several Clarksdale families as well as people throughout Coahoma and neighboring counties, including the Wingfields (among them "a lady named Laura Young," who had prisms hanging between two rooms that, he recalled in 1945, "became a play," obviously a reference to *The Glass Menagerie*); the Venables; the

Delta flood

"Wanta know something? This time tomorrow, both floors of this house will be full of floodwater. . . . The river gauge is thirty-two feet of water at Friar's Point, and the crest is still above Memphis."
(*Kingdom of Earth*)

Evangelist Gypsy Smith

"Hmm. Uh-huh—I reckon you'd never guess from me, that I was what they call saved by this preacher Gypsy Smith when he came here last spring. But I sure in hell was, I was what they calls saved, but it didn't last much longer than a cold in the head. Hmum." (*Kingdom of Earth*)

Cutrers (one of whom was named Blanche, another Stella, and a young man who married a Cutrer was drowned in nearby Moon Lake). The Bobo family in nearby Lyon provided the name for the bird who was a familiar of Goody Tutwiler, the witch in the short story "The Yellow Bird," and the nickname of one prominent local woman, Baby Doll, supplied the name of a play and one of its main characters. One of Tom's schoolmates was something of a bully named Brick Gotcher, who, along with another young man who broke his leg one night jumping over the elk statue at the Elks Hall, pro-

vided elements for the character of Brick Pollitt in *Cat on a Hot Tin Roof*. In the early part of this century a young man named Roy Flowers hopped off a freight train in Coahoma County and took a job as the bookkeeper on an enormous plantation a few miles south of Clarksdale. Within a few years he was the owner of the spread and ultimately became one of the largest cotton planters in all the Delta. Elements of that story, if not the character himself, Tennessee adapted for *Cat on a Hot Tin Roof*. Stories of other local figures, including members of the Clark and Stovall families, provided inspiration for his art. Amazingly Tennessee Williams was able to take all those diverse elements and blend them into a fascinating and original whole.

Ozzie, who became nursemaid for the two Williams children shortly after Tom's birth and continued in the position for several years, following the family to Nashville and finally Clarksdale, until 1916, also told them stories, although they were of a different kind from those he heard from the family. It was through her that Tom became conscious of the large black population of the Delta, the major labor force that picked the cotton before mechanical harvesters took away many of the jobs. Their lives were markedly different from those of Delta planters, a fact surely not lost on an impressionable young mind. When Ozzie went away one year on a visit somewhere and never returned, young Tom blamed himself, probably without justification, for her disappear-

The Elks Hall in Clarksdale, Mississippi, with the statue of an elk in front. As a young man, John Wesley Cutrer broke his leg when he attempted to leap over the elk, an event that provided Tennessee with the idea of Brick's accident when he attempted to jump the high hurdles on the football field in *Cat on a Hot Tin Roof.*

ance, because he had used a racial slur in speaking to her.

In those days in the Delta, cotton was certainly king, as it remains to this day, and it shaped the destiny of almost everyone living in the region. That Tom was acutely conscious of cotton and its effect on the Delta economy is clearly indicated by his letters. From the University of Missouri in September 1929 he would write to his grandfather in Clarksdale a complaint about the hot weather, to which he added, "But I suppose that you are willing to suffer any degree of temperature as long as it is good for the cotton." The state of the Reverend Dakin's finances apparently depended heavily on the kindness of the Delta planters to

Young Tom sits with his nurse, Ozzie, and the women folk of his family. From Ozzie, the children learned about an aspect of southern life totally different from that they knew from their family.

43

whom he ministered. A later letter, written September 1931, also from Columbia, Missouri, again demonstrates Tom's knowledge of and concern for the agricultural conditions: "I suppose the cotton situation in Mississippi is very depressing now. I hope that your income isn't suffering much from it."

The planters and their families have long had a reputation as hard-working and prosperous on the one hand but fun-loving and daring on the other. The contrast between Big Daddy, concerned with the welfare of his plantation, and his son Brick, a drinker and carouser, dramatizes that contrast most effectively. In the Delta eccentricity is not only tolerated, but even cherished, and the region is rife with stories of bizarre murders, family scandals, and crooked land deals and politics. Outsiders are often surprised that Deltans think nothing of driving one hundred miles or more to another town or plantation for a party, the promise of an afternoon or evening of fun. With many members of what we may term, with reservations, "the Delta aristocracy," the rule always seems to be "feast or famine," for when the cotton yield is large and the money flowing, they do not hesitate to spend it. "Next year," one planter said a few years ago, "may not be this good, so we'd better enjoy it while we can."

The Delta was and is essentially a closed society, with a welcome for visitors but not for outsiders, especially Yankees, planning to settle there. Many Delta residents are fiercely exclusive, disdainful of hill dwellers in the eastern part of the state—Oxford and Columbus and Tupelo—who were, traditionally, never as affluent or, as it seemed to many of the Deltans, as sophisticated as they. In his autobiography, *Lanterns on the Levee*, William Alexander Percy expresses without reservation his fear that the hill folk will move in and destroy what he saw as the Delta culture, carefully developed and nurtured through the years. Once when William Faulkner showed up intoxicated at Percy's home to play tennis, his host attributed the novelist's behavior to the fact that he was, more or less, from the wrong side of the Choctaw Ridge which separates the Delta from the hills. The Delta society was also sharply stratified, with the large black population at the bottom, a condition reflected in several of Tennessee's works. At the heart of Lady Torrance's tragedy in *Orpheus Descending* lies the fact that she is the daughter of an Italian immigrant and the man she loves, David Cutrere, is the scion of a Delta planter's family.

Despite the partying and other seemingly unintellectual or unspiritual pursuits that mark Delta life, the arts in the area have flourished for decades. Just down the road from Clarksdale is Greenville, often called, with some justification, the Athens of the South. It was a phrase Tennessee surely must have heard, since he has Alma Winemiller declare in *The Eccentricities of a Nightingale* that she wants to make her hometown of Glorious Hill "the *Athens of the Delta*." Greenville is the home of the famous Percy family, whose members in-

"Jooking" in Clarksdale

"That's where you get in a car and drink a little and drive a little and stop and dance a little to a juke box and then you stop dancing and you just drink and drive and then you stop driving and just drink, and then, finally, you stop drinking. . . .
(*Orpheus Descending*)

Production still of *Orpheus Descending*, with Lois Smith and John Marriott

"Hey, Uncle Pleasant, give us the Choctaw cry. . . . He's part Choctaw, he knows the Choctaw cry."
(*Orpheus Descending*)

clude not only the poet William Alexander but also his cousin and ward, Walker Percy, the distinguished author of novels such as *The Moviegoer* and *The Last Gentleman*. In addition, through the years there has been in the Delta an abundance not only of authors but also of painters, sculptors, musicians—and the blues, which originated there among the black population, can be heard on any given night. "Going jooking," of which Carol Cutrere speaks in *Orpheus Descending*, is a longtime and continuing Delta practice of going to juke joints to hear blues music. Carol offends the planter class to which she belongs because of her support of civil rights for the blacks and her association with the Conjure Man, who is a mixture of Choctaw and black.

On Sundays the Dakins and their extended family would after morning services often go to Moon Lake Casino for dinner (until recent decades the southern term for the midday meal), though the minister must have been aware of the reputation of the place and what had probably been going on there the night before. Certainly his grandson made use of the casino's shady reputation in his dramas twenty years later. Moon Lake, an old channel of the Mississippi River, is truly one of the most ubiquitous of the many images and symbols in Ten-

Moon Lake Casino

"Afterward we pretended that nothing had been discovered. Yes, the three of us drove out to Moon Lake Casino, very drunk and laughing all the way. . . . We danced the Varsouviana! Suddenly in the middle of the dance the boy I had married broke away from me and ran out of the casino. A few moments later—a shot!" (*A Streetcar Named Desire*)

nessee's dramas, and one can only imagine how much that backwater of the Mississippi must have impressed the young boy. The very sound of it is magical, a fact of which Tom Williams, who in his maturity would become one of the great American poetic minds of this century, was fully aware. *Moon Lake:* it rolls off the tongue like an invocation to a beautifully soothing memory of the past. Often devotees of the plays from other parts of the country who make their pilgrimage to Mississippi to witness firsthand the sites that inspired

Williams are surprised to discover that Moon Lake actually exists, having assumed that it was a convenient symbol created by the playwright to suit his dramatic needs. Of all the abiding and unforgettable symbols the playwright employed, none shimmers more in the memory or resonates more in the imagination of Williams characters.

In scenes and language surely drawn from the playwright's own youth, Amanda Wingfield, living in exile in St. Louis, recalls for her children the gloriously romantic Mississippi of her young womanhood when she attended the Delta Planters' Cotillion and her many "gentlemen callers," including "some of the most prominent young planters of the Mississippi Delta—planters and sons of planters!" One of her "bright particular beaux" was Bates Cutrer, who quarreled with "that wild Wainwright boy" and "shot it out on the floor of Moon Lake Casino." Wounded in the stomach, Bates died, leaving his widow "eight or ten thousand acres . . . ," but, Amanda insists, carrying her picture on his body when he died. Blanche DuBois, living in exile and fear in New Orleans, recalls in agony the night she and her husband Allan and his older male friend "drove out to Moon Lake Casino, very drunk and laughing all the way." They were dancing to the "Varsouviana" when suddenly, Blanche, having discovered that Allan and the friend are lovers, told him, "You disgust me," and her husband broke away from her and ran out of the casino. "A few minutes later—a shot!" She and everyone else ran out and "gathered by that terrible thing at the edge of the lake!" Then she heard voices say, "Allan! Allan! The Grey boy!" That scene, that event, and the music associated with it continue to haunt her until her mental collapse at the end of *A Streetcar Named Desire*. She drinks to clear it from her consciousness, if only temporarily, but it remains an inescapable part of her memory.

In *Battle of Angels* Beulah Binnings recalls that the father of Lady Torrance bought cheap land on the north shore of Moon Lake on which he planted fruit trees and grapevines and built wooden arbors in which people could get drunk on the wine he had made and "carry on." In good weather, Beulah recalls, she and her husband Pee Wee would go there with other young people "an' court up a storm. . . ." Although Mississippi was dry in those days, on Moon Lake they could buy and drink that "Dago red wine." With erotic detail she recalls that each of the "white wooden arbors had a lamp in it, and one by one, here and there, the lamps would go out as the couples begun to make love. . . . What strange noises you could hear if you listened, calls, cries, whispers, moans—giggles." Later, lamps relighted, Lady and her father would sing Italian songs. Today no one in the area recalls such an Italian "wine garden" on the shores of Moon Lake, but since that part of the Delta is heavily populated with a variety of ethnic groups, it is possible that Tennessee knew of such a place and of such activities.

In a passage reminiscent of the above John Buchanan in *Summer and Smoke* attempts to lure the puritanical Alma Winemiller to a romantic evening at "Moon Lake Casino where anything goes . . . ," including gambling, cockfighting, and illegal liquor. He describes private rooms, available by the hour, where they can drink Chianti and then relates to the shocked Alma how a young woman he had met at the door of the depot in Glorious Hill after she alighted from the Cannonball Express took him to the casino. Young John, naive then as Miss Alma is now, was terrified and fled. It would be inappropriate to take Alma there, he tells her, because she is the "Nightingale of the Delta" and everyone knows her, including "people you'd run into at church." Alma's father is the Episcopal rector in the town, so it is clear that Williams was drawing on his own childhood memories to recreate this "den of iniquity," of which he must have heard though surely had not experienced in his tender years. As noted above, Reverend Dakin loved a good story and enjoyed relating it, and in his grandson, he found a willing and eager listener.

Such scenes as the above, along with those in *Streetcar* and other New Orleans plays, helped to create the reputation Williams achieved in certain circles for exploiting "southern decadence." More important, however, than such a negative view of life were the positive elements he absorbed in the area, elements that his creativity was later able to convert into great literature. The casino, by the way, still stands, looking out over placid Moon Lake, that backwater of the Mississippi River, and there is still a restaurant there as well as the rooms upstairs similar to those to which John Buchanan proposes to take Miss Alma in *Summer and Smoke* and to which she takes the traveling salesman at the end of the play.

Although, as noted above, Tennessee's last sustained stay in Mississippi occurred when he was nine and although he lived in a variety of spots in the United States and abroad—New York, Key West, New Orleans, Los Angeles, Italy, Sicily—he never lost that unmistakable Delta brogue. What the Delta of his memory, as opposed to what may have been the reality, came to represent for Tennessee was the realm of happiness and comfort from which he had been evicted with his beloved sister. In Mississippi Rose had been well, happy, apparently not yet exhibiting signs of the condition that would later make her life—and the lives of other members of the family—miserable and that ultimately would result in her lobotomy. Subconsciously, Tennessee seems to have blamed most of their subsequent problems, including Rose's mental deterioration, on that displacement from the Delta.

In those early years in Clarksdale Tom Williams absorbed from his minister grandfather, his genteel grandmother Rose, his mother, and the residents of the town and county, as well as from the very atmosphere in which his days and nights were passed, a southern character and a southern mystique, which,

Tennessee Williams in New York City, c. 1945

"I'm tellin' you it's the truth, we got to face it, we're under a life-long sentence to solitary confinement inside our own lonely skins for as long as we live on this earth!"
(*Orpheus Descending*)

along with his sexual orientation, were the most important influences upon his writing. The Delta experiences he could never have had in a city, certainly not in St. Louis, and it is fortunate that his memory was a sponge, soaking up what he saw and heard long before the boy he was then could possibly have understood the implications of the material.

In the early 1940s, when his career drew him to New York City, his memory of that childhood home provided solace for the lonely stranger in a strange city. "The first night I spent in New York," he said, "I was quite lonely . . . and I was frightened," and he wrote a short play, which he described as being "about my childhood memories of Mississippi." The inspiration from that locale would continue to offer him solace for the rest of his life, despite his being physically withdrawn from it. His mother remembered his having written the following telling passage: "I assure you that the South is the country of my heart as well as my birth." He insisted that if he wrote about "Yankees," he would surely "find every bit as much 'damnation' among them— and not as much charm!" His characters, his "little people" as he called them, were indeed "not really damned" but rather redeemed by "courage and gallantry," which he identified as "important and very southern qualities, bred in

Movie still, *This Property Is Condemned*

"She is a remarkable apparition—thin as a beanpole and dressed in outrageous cast-off finery. She wears a long blue velvet party dress with a filthy cream lace collar and sparkling rhinestone beads. On her feet are battered silver kid slippers with large ornamental buckles. Her wrists and her fingers are resplendent with dimestore jewelry. She has applied rouge to her childish face in artless crimson daubs and her lips are made up in a preposterous Cupid's bow." (Production Note, "This Property Is Condemned")

The Starr Boarding House is an excellent example of a Tennessee Williams set—a dilapidated house, faded elegance crumbling into ruin, lacy wicker furniture, rambling verandas, and colorful descriptive names—all permeated by a poetic atmosphere of genteel decay.

the bones of the people I wrote about, such as Amanda Wingfield and even the little girl on the railroad tracks." The latter is, of course, a reference to Willie, the teenager in "This Property Is Condemned," who remains in the abandoned Delta boardinghouse after her sister Alma has died and her mother has abandoned her. Significantly, the only other character is a boy named Tom, and that is the play he wrote his first night in New York as he battled homesickness in the big city, remembering and yearning for his youth in the Delta.

Only on a few occasions after that fateful move to St. Louis did he return at all to the state of his birth, the first time in 1920 when he stayed with his grandparents in Clarksdale while his mother was ill. Nevertheless, Mississippi, or the memory of it, continued to affect Williams's work—consider the plays set in the Delta and *The Rose Tattoo* and *Sweet Bird of Youth*, both set on the Mississippi Gulf Coast. The early years in Mississippi, combined with the tension evident between his recollection of those times and the sorrows of the Missouri years, provided him with inspiration and material that benefited him for the rest of his life

Tennessee laughed just as heartily every time he watched the film of *Baby Doll* (starring Karl Malden, Carroll Baker, and Eli Wallach), but he never thought the film captured all the wanton hilarity in the script.

Tennessee Williams
and Elia Kazan

"Some day when time permits I would like to write a piece about the influence, its dangers and its values, of a powerful and highly imaginative director upon the development of a play. . . . Elia Kazan and I have enjoyed the advantages and avoided the dangers of this highly explosive relation-function." (Tennessee Williams, "Note of Explanation," *Cat on a Hot Tin Roof*)

Clarksdale, Mississippi, celebrated the playwright by unveiling a special commemorative United States postal stamp on October 13, 1995, the first day of issue, and followed this with comments by Williams's biographers Lyle Leverich and Dick Leavitt, Clarksdale Postmaster Lawrence Wills, and the playwright's brother, Dakin Williams, all of whom recalled humorously that Tennessee never had a stamp when he needed one. Left to right: Leavitt, Wills, Leverich, D. Williams

and career. In a 1932 letter written to his mother from the University of Missouri, he commented on the South as a source of his subject matter: of "Big Black: A Mississippi Idyll" he wrote, he was "returning to reminiscences of my native locale for inspiration. . . ." While spending the summer of 1935 in Memphis with his grandparents, he informed a friend of the abundance of "fascinating things to write about" in the South: "You should visit these southern plantations! Every one down here seems to have a history that you could write volumes about." Years later during Elia

Kazan's filming of the movie *Baby Doll* in and around a once magnificent but by then abandoned mansion in Benoit, a small Delta town, Williams returned to the place where he had hung his childhood.

Williams chose to live much of his life in the South, but he was never to live in Mississippi after those early years. It was almost as though he feared that returning to the landscape of childhood he would find it not the comforting place he had fondly remembered. A few times he professed to believe that the people of his native state hated him and even insisted, in his

Tennessee's younger brother Dakin declaims his brother's poetry during one of his annual visits to Clarksdale's Delta Festival in the little park which also honors the memory of Tennessee.

paranoia, that he was afraid to return there. Certainly the reception of his work in the South was not positive until it became clear that he, like Faulkner—yet another "prophet without honor in his own country"—was a major American author. Nevertheless, evidence of the playwright are to be found everywhere in the area, including the sites he mentions in his plays, the family names, and the stained-glass windows in St. George's Episcopal church devoted to the memory of his grandparents, the Dakins. Tennessee would also be pleased to know that Clarksdale, the town from which he derived much of his material and inspiration, memorializes him and his work with an annual Tennessee Williams Festival and with Tennessee Williams Park with an angel fountain. On 13 October 1995, the United States Post Office issued a stamp honoring Williams, with the first-day ceremonies appropriately taking place at Clarksdale. Also, thanks to Tennessee's association with the Cutrer mansion, it has been saved from demolition.

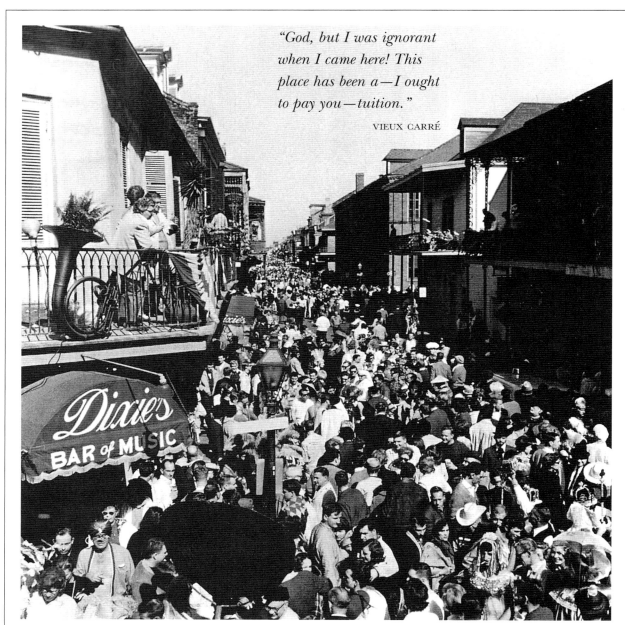

> *"God, but I was ignorant when I came here! This place has been a—I ought to pay you—tuition."*
>
> VIEUX CARRÉ

Mardi Gras, New Orleans, 1940s

One of the Last Frontiers of Bohemia

For Rose and Tom Williams the southern idyll had ended when their father became a branch manager of the International Shoe Company and moved his family to St. Louis, leaving behind Reverend and Mrs. Dakin and the quiet, somnolent small-town life of the Delta. For Tennessee the removal of his family from the "dark, wide world" of Mississippi came to represent a new expulsion from Eden into a cold northern world lacking the benefits, virtues, and social decorum he remembered. The memories of those first seven years in Mississippi, idealized by contrast with the new urban existence Tom now endured, gradually crystallized in his memory, a rich source on which he could draw for consolation and inspiration. His experiences, good and bad, served as a sort of magical catalyst to convert the past into a precious stone of memory, enriching it with a luster and magnificence it may never have possessed in reality, so that for the rest of his life, he was always searching, both as himself and in the guise of various of his characters, for such a perfect world once again.

After the family had been in St. Louis for almost a year, a third child, Dakin, was born and soon became the favorite of his father. Consequently, Tom and Rose, feeling more excluded than ever from paternal devotion, turned more and more introspective. Tom escaped the harshness of reality in his writing, first poetry and fiction and later drama, and he would publish his first story in *Weird Tales* when he was seventeen. In the meantime Rose grew progressively more disturbed, slowly losing touch with reality. The next two decades Tom spent first in St. Louis, then at the University of Missouri in Columbia, Washington University in St. Louis, and the University of Iowa. For a while, after his father, unhappy with his grades, withdrew Tom from college, he worked in the stock department at the shoe factory, a job he loathed and viewed as a punishment. This situation and its results he later dramatized in *The Glass Menagerie.*

Rose Williams, c. 1928

Valediction

She went with morning on her lips
down an inscrutable dark way
and we who witnessed her eclipse
have found no word to say.
I think our speechlessness
is not a thing she would approve,
she who was always light of wit
and quick to speak and move—

I think that she would say goodbye
can be no less a lyric word
than any song, than any cry
of greeting we have heard!

TENNESSEE WILLIAMS, <u>THE ELIOT</u>, YEAR-
BOOK OF THE UNIVERSITY OF MISSOURI

On his return to St. Louis after graduation from Iowa, Tom was shocked to discover the degree to which Rose's mental state had deteriorated. That, combined with the tense family situation, made life in the Williams home untenable. Living under the same roof with a father whose attitude toward his sensitive son fell little short of contempt, hearing the almost constant bickering of his parents, he watched in pained helplessness as his beloved sister slipped further and further away from him and into the nightmarish world of her growing hysteria that would finally lead to her being institutionalized. This combination of circumstances induced Thomas Lanier Williams to flee St. Louis in December 1938 "like a migratory bird," to use his own words, "going to a more congenial climate."

The direction he chose, not surprisingly, was south. "I have learned," he said years later, "that the further south you go in the United States, the more congenial life is." It was not to Mississippi that he returned, however—he no longer had immediate family there—but to New Orleans. Edwina Williams wrote of her son that when he set out on that journey, "I had the feeling this time, in one sense, he was never coming back to me." Those words proved prophetic, in both a real and metaphorical sense, for never again would Tom live at home for long periods of time, and when next he visited his mother, he was hardly the son who had left the shelter of her nest. That departure from St. Louis, later drama-

Lyle Saxon

"There is a writers' project here and many of the writers I have met are on it—perhaps there is room for one more. Lyle Saxon is at the head of it. . . . [He] seems very much concerned and sympathetic about my precarious situation." (*Letters*)

tized in *The Glass Menagerie*, inaugurated a pattern of restlessness and wandering—for which a bird was an appropriate image and one he often used—that would last for the rest of his life. In the 1970s Tennessee explained to Don Lee Keith that in those early years he had "trouble staying still" because young writers, whose "creative shapes have not yet been molded by their muses . . . , have trouble staying still. I did. And it isn't by chance, I think, that so many end up here in New Orleans, for short stays, at least."

Years later he recalled to Keith that on the bus that cold December, headed south, he tried "not to expect too much of his destination," then added ironically, "nothing other than salvation from the furies that had been unleashed by fate on my mortal self." In New Orleans he hoped to find a position with the Federal Writers' Project, an agency of President Roosevelt's New Deal during the Depression. The New Orleans branch, under the direction of Lyle Saxon, had been assigned the task of producing the state guide to Louisiana and the New Orleans city guide. A job for Tom never materialized, for the two guidebooks had by that time been completed and the Writers' Project had come under the critical eye of Washington politicians, but Tom's decision to settle in the Quarter proved momentous in shaping his future life and career. He had found what he was often to call in the future his "spiritual home," and in his journal he wrote on 28 December 1938, "Here surely is the place that I was *made* for if any place on this funny old world."

The next day, in a letter to his mother, he termed it "the most fascinating place I've ever been." He was amazed at the "heterogeneous" makeup of the area, with wealthy residents living next to the poor, struggling artists and writers next to laborers and businessmen. He was, he declared, enjoying living there more than any other place he had ever been. In another letter to his mother on 2 January 1939 he spoke of his love of the city, more quaint than

722 Toulouse Street, c. 1939

"Once this house was alive, it was occupied once. In my recollection, it still is, but by shadowy occupants like ghosts. Now they
enter the lighter areas of my memory." (*Vieux Carré*)

Eloi Bordelon

"He had a serious and gifted side to him, like most of
our kind. He was not a brilliant painter but he had a
distinctive and highly effective flair which later made
him a successful designer in New York." (*Letters*)

any he had seen in Europe, of the long walks
he took to Audubon Park and the beautiful
mansions in the Garden District uptown. Most
of his praise was reserved for the French Quarter, which was "alive with antique and curio
shops where some really artistic stuff is on sale,
relics of Creole homes that have gone to the
block." He found fountains, cast-iron railings,
and the courtyards with palms and poinsettias
charming, and in the French Market he was
able to buy breakfast for ten cents, a boon
given his limited budget. The shabby but genteel and romantic old French Quarter, very little affected then by progress and moderniza-
tion, had become by the 1920s a gathering
place for writers and artists, a romantic hide-
away in which to escape what problems one
might face. Rents were low, excellent food was
inexpensive—especially seafood, which Tom
relished—and an aspiring writer could meet
and commune with others of a similar bent.

For the rest of Tennessee's life the Quarter
was to remain a "place where I could catch my
breath," where he would write and enjoy the

leisurely life of the most foreign North American city. Of all the places he was to live, it was only New Orleans which elicited such lavish praise. He would later write, "If I can be said to have a home, it is in New Orleans where I've lived off and on since 1938 and which has provided me with more material than any other part of the country."

Upon his arrival in the city on 26 December 1938, Tom had presented himself to Odette and Knute Heldner, artists who knew friends of his in St. Louis and who graciously introduced him to his new environment. He accompanied them to a New Year's Eve party at which, he recalled in his *Memoirs* almost forty years later, he witnessed a decadent lifestyle that shocked him: "interesting," he wrote in his journal, but "utterly appalling." What he saw was also evidence, of course, of his imminent emancipation into a freedom that would prepare the way for the work that followed. He spent one night in a rooming house on St. Charles Avenue near Lee Circle, then moved into a hotel on Royal Street—six dollars a week—where he stayed until 1 January 1939, when he moved into a rooming house at 722 Toulouse Street. A 1940 photograph of the house shows it in a romantic state of decay, a stuccoed building with vines growing over one corner and a cast-iron second-floor balcony.

Williams's third-floor room, for which he paid ten dollars a month, opened onto a dormer window. An adjoining cubicle with a matching dormer was occupied by Eloi Borde-lon, an artist who became a close friend and, briefly, a lover. Tom wrote to Reverend and Mrs. Dakin that the house had three proprietors: a "lovely Mississippi lady" named Mrs. Anderson, Mrs. Wire, and another woman unidentified by name, although she was probably Mrs. Nesbit, the cook he writes about in another letter. The food was so good that Tom persuaded Mrs. Anderson to open a restaurant for which he provided a motto: "Meals for a Quarter in the Quarter." He hand-printed the motto on cards, distributed them in the Vieux Carré, then returned to serve as waiter, cashier, and dishwasher, thus helping to pay his rent.

Mrs. Anderson is characterized in Tennessee's letters as "a perfect termagant," who "had a hard time adjusting herself to the Bohemian spirit of the Quarter." (Mrs. Wire, the character based on her in his play "*Vieux Carré,*" curses the area as "the new Babylon destroyed by evil in the Scriptures!"). One memorable night she created havoc when the photographer who had a first-floor studio and apartment was having a party. When he ignored her complaints about the noise, she poured boiling water through holes in her kitchen floor in Tom's presence. The police were summoned and Mrs. Anderson was charged with "Malicious Mischief and disturbing the peace."

At her trial the next night at the Third Precinct police station on Chartres Street, Tom, asked by the judge if the landlady had committed the deed, responded that he "thought it was highly improbable that any lady would do such a thing!" His evasion no doubt spared his being asked to vacate his room, but embedded within it is certainly a gentle rebuke of what Mrs. Anderson had done. In a letter he wrote to his mother the following day, he reported that when they returned to the boardinghouse after the trial, Mrs. Anderson demanded to know why he had not denied that she poured the water, and when he responded that he had been under oath, the landlady replied that anyone could tell she was no lady.

The incident produced several significant results: a similar episode is described in *A Streetcar Named Desire*, and the pouring of water and subsequent trial became climactic scenes in *Vieux Carré*, the 1976 memory play in which he recreated the dramatic incidents of those important early months on Toulouse Street during which Tom was almost magically transformed into Tennessee Williams. In addition, as a result of the episode, he made the acquaintance of Mary Rose Bradford, a guest at the photographer's party, whose dress had been ruined by the water. She lived in a Creole cottage across the street from the rooming house with her husband, Roark Bradford, the night city editor for the *Times-Picayune*. He had achieved fame writing books in black dialect, including his most popular work, *Ol' Man Adam an' His Chillun* (1928), subsequently adapted by playwright Marc Connolly into the long-running Broadway hit, *Green Pastures*. The Bradfords, whose home was always a gathering place for writers—William Faulkner, Sinclair Lewis, and John Steinbeck were among those who enjoyed their hospitality through the years—introduced Tom to a visiting Broadway producer who, upon learning that he was an aspiring dramatist, offered to read his work. Characteristically Williams had mailed out all his plays and retained no copies.

Tom also became friends with another literary figure, Lyle Saxon, affectionately known as "Mr. French Quarter." Saxon was a charming man, a reporter for the *Times-Picayune*, an author, bon vivant, editor, and something of a leader of the large local gay community. The two remained friends, and a few years later Tennessee would visit the home Saxon purchased on Madison Street in the 1940s. Saxon owned a mechanical figure that played a banjo and referred to it as "my life's companion," the name Val Xavier gives to his guitar in *Orpheus Descending*. Saxon, Eloi Bordelon, and other local friends introduced Tom to all aspects of life in the Quarter, both the surface and the underground, so that for the rest of his life he felt at home there.

If Mrs. Anderson had found it difficult to adjust to the "Bohemian" Quarter, young Tom Williams reveled in it, once he became accustomed to a lifestyle completely at odds with his upbringing. The freedom afforded by New Orleans transformed him, and the tension between it and what he termed the "Puritanism" of his nature, instilled by early years living in his grandfather's rectory and the strong

Production still of *Vieux Carré*, with Richard Atfiere, Sylvia Sidney, Iris Whitney, and Olive Deering

influence of Edwina Williams—a straitlaced southern lady of the old school, who seemed to have viewed sexuality as a flaw in human nature—was to provide him with dramatic material for work he produced for the rest of his life.

The shock experienced by writers from other parts of the South and the rest of the country on their first encounter with New Orleans has often been the subject of commentary. Through the past two centuries the city has provided for many authors a tension that has contributed to the production of great literature. In William Faulkner's *Absalom, Absalom!* Mr. Compson imagines the effect on Henry Sutpen, a young man reared in rural Mississippi with its Protestant mind-set, of his

first visit to New Orleans, "that city foreign and paradoxical, with its atmosphere at once fatal and languorous, at once feminine and steelhard . . . a place created for and by voluptuousness, the abashless and unabashed senses. . . ." Much the same reaction must have been that of Tom Williams on his first exposure to a way of life almost totally alien to what he had known.

Of his 1939 stay in the Quarter, Tennessee remarked in the 1970s, "Oh, it was my first contact with a free society, I mean a bohemian world, . . . which I really encountered with a bang here." Calling it one of the "last frontiers of Bohemia," he professed to a newspaper reporter in the 1940s that he was a Bohemian, (a fact which Miss Edwina disputed when she read the article, insisting that her son ask the reporter to print a retraction). Referring to the "liberating effect" of the city, he said, "My whole personality felt free. It gave me an inner security I didn't have before. I was able to write better. I began to write with maturity." On another occasion he explained to a critic that he chose to live most of the time in Key West or New Orleans because of "the folly and fantasy in the southern temperament," which he professed to love.

Eloi Bordelon's brother, Charles Ayala, recalls the Quarter as being in those days "a little community where everybody knew everybody else," and his memories of the rooming house indicate something of how it must have affected impressionable young Tom Williams. Ayala, who was five at the time, lived with his mother in Algiers, a suburb of New Orleans, and the two of them would ride the ferry across the river every Sunday to bring Eloi a basket of food and clean clothes. Eloi was quite a contrast to the character in *Vieux Carré* based on him, the tubercular artist Nightingale, as well as to the protagonist in the one-act "Auto-Da-Fe," who bears his name. When Tom first met him, Bordelon was working as an artist for the WPA, and he later became a successful interior decorator in New York. It was Eloi who introduced the young writer to the New Orleans Athletic Club, where Tom would swim daily whenever he was in the city. One indelible impression from that time on Charles Ayala's

memory involves Mrs. Wire, one of the landladies of the complex—it is her name that Williams uses in *Vieux Carré*—whose parrot would perch on the balcony of the second floor and call out to men passing in the street below, "Come on up, boys, and have a good time." Tennessee, who was always fascinated with birds, must have been impressed by this experience.

Ironically it was a man named Jim Parrott who provided the dramatist his means of exit from the rooming house and entrance to the next phase of his life. Portrayed by Tennessee in *Vieux Carré* as an itinerant saxophonist named Sky, Parrott stayed briefly at the house before the two of them departed for a trip west, first to Texas, then to California. Parrott later was in the U.S. Air Force, then became a commercial pilot, and finally retired and settled in Florida. Tennessee, in what may have been an apocryphal story, insisted in one account of his first stay in the Quarter that because his rent was overdue, he had to slide down sheets to escape the wrath of Mrs. Anderson.

Those few months on Toulouse Street constitute one of the most crucial periods in the life of Tennessee Williams, when he was storing up material for later use, and it became the setting for the story "Angel in the Alcove" as well as the one-act "The Lady of Larkspur Lotion" and the late full-length play *Vieux Carré*. In 1939 the Musée Mécanique was operated by John Henry Hewlett and his wife, the former Lorraine Werlein, at 523 Royal Street around

Tennessee Williams and Jim Parrott

"This fellow, Jim Parrott, was driving to the West coast and invited me along
free of charge. He's a swell young fellow. . . . He's a musician and has been
promised work in Hollywood. . . ." (*Letters*)

In the attic of 722 Toulouse, c. 1979, © 1996 Christopher R. Harris

"In this old house it was either deathly quiet or else the high plaster walls were ringing like fire-bells with angry voices. . . . I had no door to my room which was in the attic, only a ragged curtain that couldn't exclude the barrage of human wretchedness often exploding." (*Vieux Carré*)

the corner from the rooming house. The Musée, a collection of charming mechanical figures and clockwork pictures, must have made a strong impression upon the young playwright, for he retained the memory of this magical place until the 1964 play *The Eccentricities of a Nightingale*, in which Mrs. Winemiller relates the story of Albertine, her sister, who with her husband, Mr. Schwarzkopf, owned the Musée Mécanique and died in the fire that destroyed it. The real Musée was closed by the Hewletts in 1939 and reopened at the World's Fair in San Francisco.

If it were possible for the twenty-seven-year-old Thomas Lanier Williams to return to the French Quarter today and see 722 Toulouse Street, he would hardly recognize it. In the 1970s it was renovated and some ill-advised alterations were instituted: the cast-iron balcony railing was replaced with wood, and a plate-glass window was installed in front of what had been the studio of the photographer. The third floor, where the young playwright launched his career, was removed, and in a poignant photo made by Christopher Harris during the 1977 renovation, Tennessee stands in the ruins of his room with the dormer window. There is no plaque to commemorate the building's significance in American literary history, but those who know the story of Tennessee's life may pause to contemplate the building and the extent to which his residence there changed the course of American drama.

In a very real sense it can be said that while Thomas Lanier Williams was born in Columbus, Mississippi, in 1911, Tennessee, his *alter ego*, was born in 1939 in a roach-infested, cramped, and romantic garret in a rooming house in the French Quarter, the spot he came to love and to call his spiritual home. Those critical months of his new existence away from St. Louis, which he had found stultifying, and from the tensions of his family life, months spent in a new and liberating environment where he could be himself and begin for the first time seriously to explore his sexual nature, served to convert the proper young man, wearing a coat and tie and polished shoes, into the Bohemian author who would ultimately blossom into a great dramatist.

Despite the new-found freedom afforded by the Quarter, Tennessee had already established the rigorous work habits that he would follow for the rest of his life, a pattern of life influenced by the religion and the Protestant work ethic that were part of his upbringing and would sustain him, giving him the discipline to work on a regular schedule, even in the "Big Easy," the American city filled with the most temptations to lure one to avoid labor in favor of indulgence in sensual pleasures. Seven days a week he rose early, drank black coffee, often at the old Morning Call, a favorite gathering place in the French Market to which characters in his plays refer, and then set to work. As a result of this controlled approach to his profession, he produced during his fifty-year writing career more than seventy plays, two novels, four books of short stories, two books of poetry, and a plethora of essays.

In an article he wrote for the *New York Times* when *Orpheus Descending* opened on Broadway, he remembers one significant event that occurred at about the time that he was residing at 722 Toulouse Street: he discovered that the Group Theatre in New York was conducting a drama contest to which he submitted four full-length plays and a collection of one-acts. The rules of contest stipulated that only authors twenty-five or younger could compete, and since Tom was twenty-eight at the time, he shaved three years off his age. The one-acts, collectively entitled "American Blues," were awarded one hundred dollars by the judges, Harold Clurman, Irwin Shaw, and Molly Day Thatcher, the wife of Elia Kazan.

Several points are significant here: the *American Blues* script was one of the first that he signed "Tennessee Williams." This was also his first contact, albeit indirect, with Kazan, who was to become the best director of his dramas in the future, and soon after the award Hume Cronyn purchased an option on *American Blues* because he considered one of the short plays, "Portrait of a Madonna," an ideal vehicle for his wife, actress Jessica Tandy. Her subsequent

The French Market and Morning Call, New Orleans

performance of that role paved the way for her legendary recreation of Blanche DuBois eight years later—and the rest is history.

There are events or moments in the lives of writers that are immeasurably significant in shaping their lives: Dante's viewing Beatrice in the streets of Florence; Shakespeare's move from Stratford to London; Melville's shipping out as a sailor in his youth; Henry Adams's encounter with the great dynamos at the 1900 World's Fair in Chicago; William Faulkner's meeting Sherwood Anderson in New Orleans. Such an element in the life of Williams was his decision, after he had failed to acquire a job with the WPA Writers Project in Chicago, to seek a similar position in New Orleans. Call it an accident, if you will, but I contend that there is more than a little truth in the old Greek concept of the divine madness which inspires poets and that there is, in the words of Shakespeare, "a tide in the affairs of men that, taken at the full, leads on to greater things."

Years afterwards Tennessee insisted that more than half of his best work had been written in New Orleans, which provided the setting for short stories ("In Memory of an Aristocrat," "Angel in the Alcove," "The Yellow Bird," "One Arm," "Hard Candy," and "The Coming of Something to the Widow Holly"); short plays ("Lord Byron's Love Letter," "The Lady of Larkspur Lotion," "Auto-da-Fe," "The Mutilated," and "Something Unspoken"); and, of course, the full-length dramas *A Streetcar Named Desire, Suddenly Last Summer*, and *Vieux Carré*. The poems inspired by the city include "Crepe de Chine," about a fortune teller on Royal Street, and "Mornings on Bourbon Street," with its impressions of places, people, and events in the Quarter.

In the short story "Angel in the Alcove" he writes that "New Orleans and the moon have always seemed to me to have an understanding between them, an intimacy of sisters grown old together, no longer needing more than a speechless look to communicate their feelings to each other." Affectionately he records how "this lunar atmosphere of the city draws me back whenever the waves of energy which removed me to more vital towns have spent themselves and a time of recession is called

for." To New Orleans he attributes a restorative effect, because "each time I have felt some rather profound psychic wound, a loss or a failure, I have returned to this city. At such periods I would seem to belong there and no place else in the country."

During these early stays he took a variety of jobs, working briefly as a waiter at both Gluck's German restaurant on Royal Street and at the Court of Two Sisters, which he converted into "The City of Two Parrots" in *Vieux Carré*. He would later recall to William Gray, an English professor Tennessee met in the 1950s when Gray was a graduate student, that he had once served as an usher at the Tudor theatre on Canal Street in the days when those uniformed employees escorted movie patrons to their seats and saw to it that order was maintained. It was an experience he was to employ as inspiration for two stories, "Hard Candy" and "The Mysteries of the Joy Rio." None of these jobs seem to have been of very long duration, and one can imagine the playwright's mind, caught up in the act of creating dramas, too distracted for such quotidian chores as showing patrons to their seats or taking orders and serving food.

In the four decades after that 1938–1939 sojourn Tennessee was drawn back again and again to the "spiritual home" with which he shared a symbiotic relationship. In the 1940s, before fame, he lived in a variety of hotels and rooming houses, mostly in the French Quarter, usually for short periods of time. Over and over again Tennessee found the "Southern

Comfort" in New Orleans. The "psychic wounds" he experienced during that decade of the 1940s included the death of his grandmother Rose Dakin and his sister's being subjected to an experimental new treatment for mental disorder, a prefrontal lobotomy. His first full-length play to be scheduled for a major production, *Battle of Angels*, opened in Boston 30 December 1940, but a series of problems doomed it from the start, and it closed after only a few performances, never making it to Broadway. Despite its failure, once that play had been produced, his career as a dramatist was more or less on course. Tennessee Williams was now a name known in Broadway circles, and soon the world, or at least that portion of it interested in theatre, would know it.

Following the trauma of the closing of *Battle of Angels*, the scathing criticism, the recriminations, and the attempts to lay blame, Tennessee fled south as far as Key West to rewrite the play. There he was reunited with Jim Parrott and for the first time met Marion Vaccaro and her family and stayed in the guesthouse of Marion's mother. Marion would become one of his best friends, his confidante, a traveling companion, and an inspiration for his work. She represented for him that "Steel Butterfly" quality he often commented on in southern women, notably Tallulah Bankhead and Carson McCullers. After the first Key West visit he returned to New Orleans, which he had by now come to think of as a haven, a place where

Tennessee and Marion Black Vaccaro, 1948

"I loved her very deeply, though perhaps not as generously as she did me. Some of my very closest friends have been women and she was one. Marion was lovely and she drank quite excessively. We traveled a lot together." (*Memoirs*)

struggling artists and writers sought and found comfort amid people of their own kind. He renewed old acquaintances in the Quarter and made new friends—among them Bill Richards, the son of the Columbus, Mississippi, physician who had delivered Thomas Lanier Williams in 1911. He joined the New Orleans Athletic Club so that he would have a place to swim, a favorite pastime, and continued to relish the

Tennessee admired Tallulah Bankhead as a survivor. Photo c. 1960.

Tennessee and Carson
McCullers, 1950

"In 1946 it was Carson
McCullers who sat at one end
of the long Nantucket work
table and I at the other, she
dramatizing *The Member of the
Wedding* and I struggling with
the tortures of the damned,
meaning Miss Alma Winemiller
of *Summer and Smoke.*"
(*Memoirs*)

inexpensive seafood in Quarter restaurants. It was during this period that he was evicted from his third-floor slave quarter apartment on the corner of Royal and Toulouse Streets as the result of an incident involving sailors who, he wrote in jest to Paul Bigelow, "come in occasionally to discuss literature with me. . . ." From the balcony he could look down upon a corner bar and feel himself to be the guardian angel of the drunks who came staggering out late at night. This seems to have been the apartment where, according to several written accounts, his first homosexual encounter in New Orleans occurred.

The Quarter provided him not only with consolation but also with the freedom to be himself. His Bohemian existence there in those early years was a functional blend of persistent, almost obsessive labor and pleasure in a new lifestyle to which he had adapted completely. He certainly knew and enjoyed the favorite local bars, the Napoleon House, for example, where he would sit on the courtyard with friends (among them Oliver Evans and William Gray, who helped him edit his first collection of poetry, *In the Winter of Cities*) in the middle of the afternoon before the evening crowd arrived. Then there was the Alpine, which would become the setting for a scene in "The Mutilated," a later play about several derelicts living in a Rampart Street rooming house —the kind of people, he notes in the stage directions, that he knew in his very first sojourn in the city. The Bourbon House, on

the corner of St. Peter and Bourbon Streets, was a favorite of writers and artists. Mystery writer Erle Stanley Gardner, who lived in the same block as the bar in the 1940s, described it as "something of a Bohemian place. . . . Quite a few of the prominent authors, playwrights, and actors ate there when in New Orleans." Although there is no record of Tennessee's ever having met the creator of Perry Mason, he must have, since they lived only a block apart and Gardner refers to "playwrights" as habitués.

There were the other bars, of course, those that catered to the kind of lifestyle that Tom had found decadent on his first exposure to it in 1938 but had subsequently embraced. On Exchange Alley were several gay bars: Ivan's, an all-night establishment with a shady reputation, and between Iberville and Canal, the even more notorious Society Page. Where Royal Street meets Canal there was Monkey Wrench Corner, a generic name in all port cities, according to Lyle Saxon, for favorite meeting places for sailors and merchant seamen. Traditionally they referred to each other as monkeys and would sometimes put a "wrench" on one another for a loan. It was in a bar on Monkey Wrench Corner that Tennessee again met Oliver Evans, whom he had first encountered in Provincetown. Evans was the poet and Tulane professor who was to become his lifelong friend, and he and Marion Vaccaro were the models for Billy and Cora in the story "Two on a Party." It was probably Monkey

538 Royal Street, 1941 (above)

"I have a room on Royal, right opposite the gay bar—The St. James, so I can hover like a bright angel over the troubled waters of homosociety. And I have a balcony and everything but a mantilla to throw across it." (*Letters*)

Exchange Alley,
New Orleans, c. 1940s

In *Vieux Carré*, Nightingale tells his "first cousin," "Go to the American Hotel on Exchange Alley just off Canal Street, and I will drop in at noon tomorrow—cousin."

Tennessee, Irene Selzneck, and Oliver Evans, "the Professor," c. 1947. Tennessee's friendship with Evans lasted until Evans's death in the late 1970s.

Wrench Corner the author describes in the short story "One Arm," in which Oliver Winemiller, a young hustler, waits for the men who will contract for his sexual services "on a certain corner of Canal Street and one of those streets that dive narrowly into the ancient part of the city." On Chartres Street there was the notorious Starlite Lounge, to which Carol Cutrere refers several times in *Orpheus Descending*. Presumably it was here that she and her cousin met Val Xavier, the protagonist of that play, during his career as a hustler. Finally, there was Dixie's Bar of Music on Bourbon, presided over by Irma and Dixie Fasnacht, sisters who became friends of Tennessee.

That peculiar mixture of types that was and to some extent still is the population of the Vieux Carré, that gumbo of people from a variety of ethnic groups, occupations, social classes, those with what is popularly termed "alternate lifestyles," in terms of sexuality and religion, living in close proximity to the more conventional denizens of the area—all of this appealed to Tennessee as no other place ever would. In the 1970s he recalled for Don Lee Keith a day "two dozen summers ago" when he and a friend met Ruthie the Duck Girl, who has been a Quarter character for close to half a century, coming out of Jackson Square. As was her habit, she asked them for two cigarettes, "one for now, one for later," and the playwright observed of the scene that "in New York, eccentrics, authentic ones, are ignored. In Los Angeles, they're arrested. Only in New Orleans

The Starlite Lounge
was a notorious hustler bar
in New Orleans.

"I'm thirty years old
and I'm done with the crowd
you run with and the places
you run to. The Club
Rendezvous, the Starlite
Lounge, the Music Bar, and all
the night places." (*Orpheus
Descending*)

are they permitted to develop their eccentricities into art." A few years later, when Keith reminded Tennessee of the remark, he said, "If that's what I said, I'll claim it and be glad to. It certainly reflects my feelings about most of my professional compatriots. . . ."

Although it was the French Quarter and its environs which would serve as the setting and inspiration for most of his New Orleans work, he was not unaware of other areas. He had friends in the uptown Garden District with its grand mansions, big front yards, and, as its name implies, beautiful gardens. One work, a composite of two plays, "Something Unspoken" and *Suddenly Last Summer*, he titled "Garden District," since both plays were set in that region. The first, a short one-act with two char-

Ruthie the Duck Girl, a French Quarter
character for four decades

acters, an imperious uptown matron and her female companion, is a unique combination of the serious, involving the strange and finally unexplained relationship between the two women, and the comic, involving the matron's desire to be Regent of the Confederate Daughters. The second play, *Suddenly Last Summer*, which is often performed alone, is a dark portrayal of the dehumanizing quality of the failure to love and to respect other human beings. Here the Garden District is portrayed as a threatening and smothering environment, representing the stifling life or propriety he had fled when he came to the Vieux Carré.

The fame and financial security that came with the premiere of *The Glass Menagerie*, 26 December 1944, and its subsequent New York opening in no degree altered Tennessee's devotion to New Orleans. The lean years were over: no longer would he have to live in such places as the roach-infested room on Bourbon Street he describes in his journals, in the story "In Memory of an Aristocrat," and in the short play "The Mutilated." Evelyn Soulé Kennedy, an author of radio dramas, remembered her husband's bringing Tennessee to their St. Ann Street house in the 1940s after the two men had struck up a conversation on the streets in typical French Quarter fashion. Mr. Kennedy had learned that Tennessee was a dramatist and knew that his wife would want to meet him. "I fed him red beans and rice," Evelyn Kennedy recalled years later, "and he loved it. He had a kind of lean and hungry look in those

days, and from then on, he would come by on occasion for a meal—soup or gumbo or whatever was at hand." Once when he was there, two women friends of the Kennedys, unaware of his identity, complained that they had seen *The Glass Menagerie* in New York and had no idea what it was about. "Why don't you ask the author," Mrs. Kennedy inquired, indicating Tennessee, much to the chagrin of the two playgoers.

In 1946 the dramatist, successful and famous by then as a result of the staging of *The Glass Menagerie*, resided briefly in the Pontchartrain Hotel on St. Charles Avenue while waiting for an apartment in Dick Orme's house on St. Peter Street to become available. He soon found, however, that the uptown area lacked the freedom and congeniality of the Quarter and moved into a second-floor apartment on Orleans Avenue across from the old Quadroon Ballroom building. In a letter to Donald Windham he described the apartment as haunted, but he decided that the ghost was a friendly one, and he loved the balcony there because it offered a view of the statue of Christ in the garden behind St. Louis cathedral, His arms lifted as if to comfort the whole world. It was to remain Tennessee's favorite view in the city for the rest of his life. It was here that he gave the infamous party for uptown debutantes who were shocked to discover his sleeping arrangements with Pancho Rodriguez y Gonzales, with whom he was living at the time.

When the third-floor apartment in Dick

710 Orleans Avenue,
New Orleans, 1946

St. Louis Cathedral, viewed from the rear

"It had a lovely gallery and sitting out there on that gallery I could see in the garden
behind the cathedral the great stone statue of Christ, his arms outstretched as if
to invite the suffering world to come to him." (*Memoirs*)

Orme's building at 632 St. Peter was finally vacated, Tennessee and Pancho moved into what he would call his favorite apartment. There was a skylight under which he sat daily at a refectory table to work on *Summer and Smoke*. He soon abandoned that play, however, to return to one which had gone through various working titles, including *Blanche's Chair in the Moon* and *The Poker Night*. From the apartment, he later recalled, he could hear that "rattletrap streetcar named Desire" that ran through the Quarter, "up one old narrow street and down another" and the one named Cemeteries running along Canal Street six blocks away. "It seemed to me an ideal metaphor for the human condition," he wrote, and therefore the name of the play as well as Blanche DuBois's famous opening lines—"They told me to take a street-car named Desire, and then transfer to one called Cemeteries and ride six blocks and get off at—Elysian Fields!"— evolved from his location. In *Streetcar* he placed the Kowalski apartment at 632 Elysian Fields, a building that bears no resemblance to the stage directions in the text, but it seems clear that he merely took the number 632 from St. Peter Street, where he wrote the masterpiece, and transferred it to Elysian Fields, a street name which suited his metaphoric pattern: Desire to Cemeteries to Elysian Fields: life to death to the afterlife. However, the location he describes—the street running between the river and the L & N tracks by the river and the raffish charm of the place—clearly is the

Tennessee, in the apartment at 710 Orleans Street, c. 1945

"All that I distinctly remember writing at that time in the French Quarter was a strange little play called *Ten Blocks on the Camino Real*." (Memoirs)

Faubourg Marigny, the second oldest part of the city, just downriver from the Vieux Carré. It is noteworthy that as late as the 1940s, guidebooks still identified that triangular area as part of the French Quarter.

If Blanche DuBois should return to New Orleans from whatever haven has sheltered her for the last half century and attempt to follow those directions today, she would be perplexed indeed. The streetcar named Desire was re-

Tennessee and Pancho
Rodriguez, c. 1941

"[Pancho Rodriguez] relieved
me, during that period, of my
greatest affliction, which is perhaps the major theme of my
writing, the affliction of loneli-
ness that follows me all my
days and nights." (*Memoirs*)

632 St. Peter Street, c. 1946

"What I liked most about it was a long refectory table under a skylight which
provided me with ideal conditions for working in the mornings. I know of no city
where it is better to have a skylight than New Orleans." (*Memoirs*)

"Physical beauty is passing. A transitory possession. But beauty of the mind and richness of the spirit and tenderness of the heart—and I have all of those things—aren't taken away, but grow! Increase with the years! How strange that I should be called a destitute woman! When I have all of these treasures locked in my heart."

A STREETCAR NAMED DESIRE

Jessica Tandy, as Blanche DuBois

The streetcar named Desire in 1948 on the last day
it made its way through the French Quarter

"They told me to take a streetcar named Desire,
and then transfer to one called Cemeteries
and ride six blocks and get off at—Elysian Fields."
(*A Streetcar Named Desire*)

nation, since the playwright rearranged the topography of reality to accommodate his expressionistic vision. Ironically, the avenue named Elysian Fields in no way reflects the eternal state of bliss its name implies and never even came close to matching the dream of the man who named it, Bernard de Marigny, and his vision of a Champs Elysees for New Orleans the equal of that in Paris. Certainly for Blanche life there proved to be anything but heavenly. Even today, however, Blanche would still hear "those cathedral chimes," which remain perhaps "the cleanest thing in the Quarter."

During that lengthy (for him) stay on St. Peter Street in 1946–1947, Tennessee worked from early morning until he was, as he recalled in his *Memoirs*, "spent with the rigors of creation," then went around the corner to Victor's Restaurant where he would drink a Brandy Alexander, eat a sandwich, and listen to Ink Spots recordings on the jukebox. Afterwards he would stroll the seven blocks to the New Orleans Athletic Club on Rampart Street to swim in its indoor pool. Some afternoons he sat in Jackson Square, where he met and became friends with Lorraine Werlein, who, with her former husband, had owned the Musée Mécanique when Tom had visited it in 1939. She recalls that in the 1940s the two of them would commiserate with each other on the pains of a writer's existence: "Unfortunately for me, I was at work on a novel that would never be published, but he was writing his greatest play."

It was around this time, either during his

placed by buses in 1948. If Blanche boarded the bus named Desire and transferred to the bus named Cemeteries on Canal Street, she would wind up in the graveyard itself rather than the immortal fields of glory envisioned by the Greeks. Of course, even if she had in reality followed those directions in 1947, taking the appropriate streetcars as she had been instructed, she would not have reached her desti-

Movie still of *A Streetcar Named Desire* with Vivien Leigh, as Blanche, and Marlon Brando, as Stanley

Victor's Café, New Orleans

"I would work from early morning to early afternoon, and then, spent from the rigors of creation, I would go around the corner to a bar called Victor's and revive myself with a marvelous drink called a Brandy Alexander, which was a speciality of the bar. I would always play the Ink Spots' rendition of 'If I Didn't Care' on the jukebox while I drank the Alexander."
(*Memoirs*)

work on *Streetcar* or after its opening on Broadway, that Tennessee and several of his friends went to Pennyland, an arcade in the first block of Royal Street in the Quarter. There they recorded seven cardboard disks, on which they told bawdy jokes, enacted a parody of a scene from *Streetcar*, recited poetry, sang popular songs, and spoke graphically of the gay life in the area. In 1999 these recordings became one of the "Lost and Found Sound" segments produced by Nikki Silva and Davia Nelson for public radio's "All Things Considered."

His grandfather Dakin often came for lengthy stays with the playwright and his companion Pancho and relished the everyday, laidback life of the Quarter. The old man also enjoyed the night parades that in the 1940s still rumbled along Royal Street during Carnival season. Tennessee's poem "Mornings on Bourbon Street" memorializes life in the Quarter at the time, describing Jackson Square and the winos and pigeons who seek shelter under arches of the Cabildo during a storm, then stumble out into the sunshine when the rain has ceased. The one-act "Lord Byron's Love Letter" portrays an earlier Carnival in the

While working on *Streetcar*, Tennessee was overjoyed when his grandfather Dakin came to live with him. The old gentleman loved the Quarter, the food, and, most of all, being with his grandson, with whom he had a strong bond. Photo c. 1948.

French Quarter in which an elderly woman, who in her youth had met the English poet on the steps of the Acropolis, now lives in poverty on Royal Street with her granddaughter, the two attempting to support themselves by showing tourists the love letter Byron had written her.

The dramatist remained on St. Peter Street for the better part of two years, before moving on when wanderlust seized him again. By then he was spending much of his time in Key West, where his friends included Marion Vaccaro and her family. (Marion and her mother, Mrs. Black, also kept an apartment in the Lower Pontalba building on Jackson Square, where she entertained the cast of the road company of *The Glass Menagerie* during their New Orleans engagement.) In 1950 Tennessee bought a conch cottage in Key West, yet another congenial southern place that would provide inspiration for his works and solitude for him to create them. By that time he and Pancho Rodriguez had separated, and he was living with Frank Merlo, a young man whose Sicilian background would inspire *The Rose Tattoo*, a drama dedicated to him. The relationship with Frank was the longest sustained one of Tennessee's life.

Marion Vaccaro

"[Marion] was a great enthusiast for all kinds of betting, and I often accompanied her and her mother to the New Orleans race track. In New Orleans they lived in a lovely apartment of the Pontalba Buildings alongside Jackson Square. When the touring company of *Menagerie* came to town, Marion and Miss Clara threw a lavish party for them." (*Memoirs*)

Tennessee and Frank Merlo, Key West, c. 1950

"As long as Frank was well, I was happy. He had a gift for creating a life and, when he ceased to be alive, I couldn't create a life for myself. So I went into a seven-year depression." (*Memoirs*)

During the decades following World War II he would see the Vieux Carré transformed from what in the short story "In Memory of an Aristocrat" he called "the cheapest and most comfortable place in America for fugitives from economic struggle." As more businesses moved into the area and many of the older residents died or moved elsewhere, it became progressively difficult for struggling artists and writers to find affordable rooms or apartments. Gentrification would set in, and by the 1970s the Vieux Carré was for the most part a high-rent area, much more a haven for tourists than struggling authors, but it continued to draw him back and to inspire him, though he grieved for some of the elements of Bohemianism that had been lost. It remained, as he told Sidney Pollack, "this crazy broken-down city" that he loved.

When Tennessee returned to New Orleans during the 1950s and 1960s, he usually checked into hotels: the Maison de Ville was one of his favorites, but he stayed there only if he could have room number nine, a lovely somewhat secluded nook in the slave quarter, small but charming, overlooking a patio with a fountain; and the Royal Orleans, where a suite has since been named in his honor. In 1951 he and his grandfather, who was in his nineties by then, resided at the Monteleone Hotel for three weeks, and when they checked out, discovered that Mr. Monteleone had taken care of their bill, no doubt in acknowledgment of the success of *Streetcar* four years earlier. Ten-

Maison de Ville, New Orleans

nessee had also mentioned the Monteleone two years earlier in *The Rose Tattoo*, in which Bessie and Flora are planning to come to New Orleans for an American Legion convention in the hopes of meeting men.

Reverend Dakin was something of a bon vivant, and in his later years his grandson's financial success enabled him to enjoy life to the fullest. His major pleasures included New Orleans food and drink (Manhattans were his favorite cocktails), and the two of them often

Kim Hunter, the original Stella, with Kenneth Holditch at Tennessee's table in Galatoire's, the playwright's favorite New Orleans restaurant.

dined at famous Creole restaurants Antoine's and Arnaud's. The owner of Arnaud's, the legendary and flamboyant Germaine Cazenave Wells, had become a good friend of Tennessee's and Pancho's. Often the playwright and a group of friends would dine and drink there late into the night, and Germaine, who had aspired to be a stage or screen actress, would entertain them with stories and songs from Broadway musicals.

It was for Galatoire's Restaurant, however, that Tennessee reserved his greatest praise, Galatoire's which he commemorated in *A Streetcar Named Desire* when Stella tells Stanley that on his poker night, she is taking Blanche there to dine. Tennessee's favorite table was in a semi-secluded corner nook in the front from which he could observe the action all over the dining room. The late Yvonne Galatoire re-

called that when her father, Justin Galatoire, was the proprietor, he would often sit with Tennessee, and the two would carry on long conversations. In 1999 Kim Hunter, who had played Stella in the original Broadway production and the movie, on her first visit to the restaurant her dialogue had helped to make famous, was entertained at Tennessee's chosen table.

In 1961 Tennessee bought the six-unit townhouse at 1014 Dumaine Street that sits on the key lot of the block, but it was another decade before he furnished the main apartment on the second floor, after which it became for the rest of his life his residence whenever he was in New Orleans. Since 1938 he had lived in an astounding variety of places in New Orleans, from roach-infested rooms on Toulouse Street and Bourbon Street to the elegant Pontchartrain Hotel to the quaintly charming Maison de Ville and, finally, in 1971, to his own house in one of the quieter residential parts of the Vieux Carré. Behind the main house there are slave quarters and a kitchen building and behind them a large pool, and although he continued to avail himself of the indoor pool at the New Orleans Athletic Club, he could also swim at home, even late at night. Tenants of his apartments during those years recalled seeing him even in cold weather come to the patio in a swimsuit and fur coat, which he would throw off before swimming a couple of laps. He could often be seen in the neighborhood, walking alone or with friends. On oc-

Tennessee's house, 1014 Dumaine Street, New Orleans

"I hope to die in my sleep, when the time comes, and I hope it will be in the beautiful big brass bed in my New Orleans apartment." (*Memoirs*)

above Marti's in the afternoon to indulge in a favorite pastime, playing poker. He occasionally had lunch or dinner at the Quarter Scene, a café two blocks from his apartment, to which he took his own bottle of wine, usually Valpolicello, since they had no liquor license. The pattern of his days was surprisingly regimented for one whose life in many areas was characterized by disorder. After working all morning, as had been his custom all his adult life, he would go out for lunch, then tour the Quarter that he had loved for over four decades. Clarke Hawley, who was at the time captain of the *Natchez*, recalled that when the playwright visited the steamship, he gave him a tour and took him up into the wheelhouse. With his usual wry sense of humor Tennessee asked after a while, "Now tell me, Captain, what about all this Mark Twain crap." In the evenings he would often dine in one of his favorite old-line restaurants and sometimes make the rounds of the bars. A special favorite was Lafitte's Blacksmith Shop, where he could sit at the piano and request old Broadway tunes from Lillie Hood, who had performed there for years. In short, the area became Tennessee's home.

During the decade of the 1970s he was interviewed several times in New Orleans, once by Dick Cavett for his television show. The two sat on the patio of the Maison de Ville, then rode a carriage through the Quarter and strolled around Jackson Square. In 1977 he was interviewed by David Chandler for an article in *People* magazine, for which Christopher

casion he did his own washing in a laundromat on the corner of Burgundy and Dumaine.

At Marti's restaurant across the street from his house, he dined on dishes the chefs prepared especially for him—vegetables cooked southern style, for example, and his favorite seafood—and sometimes he sat on the balcony

Tennessee often dined at Marti's Restaurant near his Dumaine Street apartment. One of his favorite pastimes was playing poker on the balcony of the restaurant.

R. Harris made the most remarkable series of photos of the playwright in his "spiritual home" ever to be filmed. The group went into 722 Toulouse, which was being remodeled; they sat on the patio of the Court of the Two Sisters, where he had briefly been a waiter in the early 1940s; in Jackson Square he shooed the pigeons away from Andrew Jackson's statue; and in a photo made in front of Preservation Hall, Tennessee showed obvious delight as he talked to some of the old jazz musicians. The series of pictures is a testament to the fact that for the dramatist the French Quarter was indeed home. It was also during the 1970s that the city of New Orleans set up a Desire streetcar display in the French Market and Tennessee was photographed with Don Lee Keith

Lafitte's Blacksmith Shop, New Orleans

Tennessee at the Court of Two Sisters, c. 1977. In the early 1940s, Tennessee worked briefly as a waiter in the restaurant, and he refers to it in *Vieux Carré* as "The City of Two Parrots." © Christopher R. Harris.

"Oh, they have a nice patio there, you know, palm trees and azaleas when in season. . . . There are a lot of great eating places in New Orleans, . . . lovely old mansions, you know, converted to restaurants with a gracious style . . . haunted by dead residents, of course, but with charm." (*Vieux Carré*)

Tennessee in Jackson Square,
New Orleans (above),
© Christopher R. Harris

"He thought of the tall iron
horseman before the Cabildo,
tipping his hat so gallantly
toward old wharves, the mist
of the river beginning to climb
about him." ("Mornings on
Bourbon Street")

On St. Peter Street,
Tennessee and several members of the Preservation Hall
band standing in front of the
building in which they played,
© Christopher R. Harris

Tennessee posed in 1982 with the cast of the musical *One Mo'Time*, created by and starring Vernel Bagneris. The musical was first produced by Lyle Leverich at the Toulouse Theatre in New Orleans. It also starred Lillian Boutté, who would later perform at Tennessee's memorial service at St. Louis Cathedral. The blues music of the play must have reminded Tennessee of his early years in the Mississippi Delta.

behind the controls. Keith recalled that Tennessee jokingly asked him, "What do you say to a streetcar? Giddyap?"

Tennessee Williams was constantly renewing his love-affair with the New Orleans where, he was to attest near the end of his life, he wrote more than fifty percent of his best work. The city had provided him with inspiration and material, a debt he repaid more than amply by making his vision of New Orleans a permanent part of the literary map of American. He observed to Don Lee Keith late in his life, "Writers are, as you know, the purest in spirit of all vagabonds. Especially young writers, those whose creative shapes have not yet been molded by their muses. They have trouble staying still. I did. And it isn't by chance, I think, that so many end up here in New Orleans, for short stays, at least. Then they go somewhere else and bide their time until their New Orleans seed begins to sprout. Meanwhile, this place just waits for more of them to come and go. And they do." Shortly after the success of *A Streetcar Named Desire*, a friend remarked to him that for the rest of his life there would never be a night when the play was not being staged somewhere in the world. That prophecy proved true, and even now productions of *Streetcar* abound; every time the curtain comes up on the magic of that modern tragedy, the

Tennessee met Lyle Leverich in 1978 when the producer staged *Outcry* at his Showcase Theatre in San Francisco in tandem with *Menagerie*. Earlier, Leverich had written a letter to the *New York Times* defending the playwright, which had so impressed Williams that he insisted Leverich write his biography.

New Orleans of the mind comes alive again for new audiences and new generations of play-goers. Surely the image that most people have of the city still comes from having seen a live performance or the movie or from having read *Streetcar*.

In January 1979 Tennessee gave his only public performance in the city he had called home for forty years. At the time he commented on what he saw as the unpleasant changes to the Quarter that had occurred in recent decades, including the increasing sleazi-ness of Bourbon Street, the loss of permanent residents to businesses, and the influx of tourists that made walking through the streets of some areas increasingly difficult. He seemed almost to echo Eloi Bordelon from an early one-act play, "Auto-Da-Fe," who ranted to his mother about the corruption of the area. Simi-larly, Tennessee's own mother, Miss Edwina, had written in her memoirs of her son's early days in the Big Easy, where he "became ac-quainted with a new kind of life in the French Quarter, one of wild drinking, sexual promis-cuity and abnormality." Tom Williams had early on adapted very well to that lifestyle, and now, ironically, he seemed to be echoing his mother's opinions.

After the 1979 performance at the Theatre for the Performing Arts in which Tennessee read from his work and that of his old New Or-leans friend Oliver Evans and was interviewed on stage, a small group of us who were in-volved in the event accompanied the play-wright across Rampart Street to a popular restaurant named Jonathan, where the owners hosted a dinner in his honor. In the course of that leisurely meal—Tennessee was much more relaxed than he had been before his per-formance—I inquired as to how long he would be in town, and he responded, "Not long. Car-nival season is upon us. Too many people and too much noise." He again complained about the increased sleaziness of Bourbon Street and

Why do I want to go away?
I don't have no reason to stay.
Do this, do that, they name the hour.
My heart is in a tall clock tower,
and keeps striking hours that say:
"Time for you to slide away."
What should I do? Of course, obey!
And there's no profit in delay.
Never mind No. 1202
(I think the number is thirteen)
Going, going, almost gone—
Done my bit and travelled on.

A pensive Tennessee Williams, 1960s

Only a few weeks before his death, Tennessee wrote this hauntingly prophetic poem.
No. 1202 is the number of the Sunset Suite in the Hotel Elysée where he died.

the loss of many of the romantic elements that had once made the Vieux Carré a haven for writers and artists. Over a period of almost half a century he had seen radical changes in the place that had provided him shelter and comfort as there had been changes in his work and its reception. Within a few days after the performance he had indeed departed for Key West, where his life was quieter, more secluded.

In 1983 he paid his last visit to the Dumaine Street house and the French Quarter, the place he once called "a vagabond's paradise." At the time he was arranging to sell the building, which was a problem to manage at a distance, but he planned to keep a lifetime lease on his apartment. During that visit he met with Lyle Leverich, the friend he had chosen as his biographer. A few weeks later the great playwright died, in the seventy-second year of his life, far from the congenial South he had loved, far from the sites that had inspired him.

Tennessee Williams had written in his 1975 *Memoirs*, "I hope to die in my sleep, when the time comes, and I hope it will be in the beautiful big brass bed in my New Orleans apartment." It was, alas, not in his apartment on Dumaine, as he has hoped, that he died, but in the Hotel Elysée in New York. Due to conflicting reports by the coroner and others the death, which was probably accidental, remains shrouded in mystery. He was buried, not at sea as he had wished—orally but not in his will—but in St. Louis, beside his mother in Calvary

In Beverly Hills, shortly before his death, Tennessee was photographed outside the theatre after the closing performance of *Vieux Carré*.

"It's always for everyone the time of roses! The rose is the heart of the world like the heart is the—heart of the—body!" (*The Rose Tattoo*)

Cemetery. The day of his death the tenant of the apartment in which he had written the final version of *A Streetcar Named Desire* placed a wreath and a note on the door of the building and the Louisiana Historical Society draped the Streetcar Named Desire exhibit behind the old U.S. Mint with black bunting. A month after his death a memorial service was held in New Orleans's St. Louis Cathedral, which he

Tennessee stands beside the St. Louis Cathedral, 1977. © Christopher R. Harris.

"Those cathedral bells— they're the only clean thing in the Quarter." (*A Streetcar Named Desire*)

Tennessee Williams is buried near his mother in Calvary Cemetery, with space left between them for his sister Rose, who would survive him by sixteen years.

"The violets in the mountains have broken the rocks."
(*Camino Real*)

On 26 February 1983, the morning Tennessee Williams died, a large crowd gathered outside The Hotel Elysée. He had always referred to death as "The Sudden Subway."

Entrance to Calvary Cemetery, St. Louis, Missouri

"They're disappearing behind me. Going. People you've known in places do that: they go when you go. The earth seems to swallow them up, the walls absorb them like moisture, remain with you only as ghosts; their voices are echoes, fading but remembered. . . . This house is empty now."

VIEUX CARRÉ

The day Tennessee died, Frenchy (Marcel DeNievre), a resident of 632 St. Peter Street, where Williams had written *Streetcar* more than three decades before, placed a black wreath on the door.

On the day of Tennessee's death George Jordan, art director of the *Times-Picayune,* draped the Louisiana Historical Society's streetcar named Desire.

hibit at the Old Mint, set up in the 1970s, was removed a few years ago, supposedly for repairs, and it seems unlikely that it will ever be restored. There is a plaque on the St. Peter Street house where much of *Streetcar* was written, but it identifies the site as the home of a nineteenth-century artist, long forgotten, and almost as an afterthought adds that in 1946 and 1947, American's greatest playwright also resided there. The rented rooms and apartments and hotels in which he lived and wrote, however, the restaurants in which he dined, and the bars in which he drank and celebrated with friends—many of these remain and evoke his spirit. Indeed, wherever one turns in the French Quarter, the memory of the man and his work may be rekindled, and the chimes of St. Louis Cathedral, still ring out their clear and clean notes onto the Quarter air.

The only real, full-sized streetcars running these days are on the St. Charles line, but the ghost of that rattletrap old streetcar named Desire surely still runs through the Quarter of memory, past all those landmarks Williams held so dear. In truth, he re-created a French Quarter of the imagination—that is the Quarter that legions of his fans remember, the Quarter which countless theatregoers and readers of his work all over the world believe to be real. Buried though he may be in St. Louis, a city he professed to dread, his sometimes restless spirit must still wander the narrow old streets of the Vieux Carré, which he made a permanent and unforgettable part of the liter-

immortalized in *A Streetcar Named Desire* with one of Blanche's final lines: "Those cathedral bells, they're the only clean things in the Quarter." Following her death in 1996 his beloved sister Rose was buried beside him.

The physical evidence of Tennessee's life in New Orleans is sparse. The Desire streetcar ex-

New Orleans memorial service for Tennessee, St. Louis Cathedral:
(left to right) actress Sylvia Miles, who read from *Vieux Carré*; Father Gerald
Barrett; Rev. Sidney Lanier, Tennessee's cousin; the late George DeVille; singer
Lillian Boutté; Lyle Leverich; and Kenneth Holditch.

ary history of the world in *A Streetcar Named Desire* and other works. Turn the corner into any narrow street lined with those crumbling old buildings, some still inhabited by the dispossessed souls he cherished and immortalized, and it should not surprise you if you suddenly encounter him, wearing one of the southern "costumes" that he fancied, perhaps a seersucker or white linen suit and a panama hat, surveying through those large tortoise shell glasses the domain to which he has established permanent title.

En Avant

From all these southern experiences—
the childhood in the Mississippi hills
and the Delta, the years moving back
and forth from New Orleans to Key West (he
never stayed put in one place for very long and
described himself as being always in flight in
the hopes of escaping the past and finding
something better)—Tennessee drew most of
the material that he was to transform through
the magic of his talent into great literature. To
criticism that his portrayal of the region was
not accurate, not realistic, he replied once that
he was not a sociologist but a dramatist. "What
I am writing about is human nature," he said. "I
write about the South because I think the war
between romanticism and the hostility to it is
very sharp there." He was not a realist, but as
Harold Clurman pointed out, "the intensity
with which he feels whatever he does feel is so
deep, is so great, that we do end up with a
glimpse of another kind of reality; that is, the
reality in the spirit rather than in society."

In *Twelfth Night* Shakespeare wrote, "Some
are born great, some achieve greatness, and
some have greatness thrust upon them." In
Tennessee Williams's case it would seem that
perhaps all three contributed their share to
making him America's major playwright.
Thomas Lanier Williams was born in Mississippi at almost the same time that the Southern
Renaissance was blossoming into being. Addi-
tionally, he had the advantage of being part of
a family of talkers and storytellers and readers,
blessed with the southern love of language,
words for words' sake. Surely some conjunc-
tion of planets occurred at his birth so that
from even the agonizing realities of his family
life—his parents' marital problems, his father's
treatment of him, and his sister's mental insta-
bility—he made sweet use, turning them
through the magic of his creativity into great
art.

That he *achieved* greatness was in no small
part due to the tenacity and ardor with which
he worked; his Calvinist forebears might have
found much to criticize in his work and his life,

but they could not have faulted him in his devotion to the Puritan work ethic. During the most productive period of his life—and he never truly stopped working—he was writing feverishly for five to eight hours a day, every day, in fact, except Easter, when he always rested, he said, a habit he retained from his proper childhood in Episcopal rectories. Even in the later years when he was older and tired and depressed by the bitter denunciation he experienced at the hands of several American critics, he was still writing, creating new works or revising old, for he was never completely satisfied with any of his dramas, save perhaps *A Streetcar Named Desire*. There is no greater gift one can give a writer, he believed, than the blessing of a good day's work.

Greatness was *thrust* upon him, I believe, by the fact—be it accident or cosmic design—that his being southern provided him with an inherent mass of material—and by his having chosen to move to New Orleans in 1938, where the proper young Episcopalian named Tom with his straitlaced upbringing was converted into Tennessee through the alchemy of his initiation into the freedom of the French Quarter.

So we can thank the gods—the Muses if you will—for those qualities he inherited from his parents and grandparents; that he did not falter in the face of adversity but transformed it into art; and that his strong sense of place, southern place, the Mississippi Delta and New Orleans specifically, which gave him a sense of identity, also provided such an abundance of inspiration and material and, yes, Southern Comfort for the playwright.

*"The fire's gone out of the day
but the light of it lingers."*

CAMINO REAL

CREDITS

Permission to quote from unpublished material by Tennessee Williams courtesy of the University of the South, Sewanee, Tennessee.

Excerpts from *Memoirs* of Tennessee Williams quoted by special permission of the University of the South, Sewanee, Tennessee.

Grateful acknowledgment is made to New Directions Publishing Corp., for the use of excerpts from the following works by Tennessee Williams: *Camino Real* by Tennessee Williams, from *Camino Real*, copyright © as "Camino Real," revised and published version, © 1953 by The University of the South, renewed 1981 by The University of the South; *Cat on a Hot Tin Roof*, copyright © 1954, 1955, 1971, 1975 by The University of the South; *Eccentricities of a Nightingale*, copyright © 1948, 1964 by The University of the South; *The Glass Menagerie*, copyright © 1945 by The University of the South and Edwin D. Williams; *The Night of the Iguana* and *Sweet Bird of Youth*, from *The Theatre of Tennessee Williams*, Vol. IV, copyright © 1972 by The University of the South; *Rose Tattoo* and *Summer and Smoke*, from *The Theatre of Tennessee Williams*, Vol. II, copyright © 1971 by The University of the South; *A Streetcar Named Desire*, copyright © 1947 by The University of the South; *27 Wagons Full of Cotton*, copyright © 1945 by The University of the South; *Vieux Carrè*, copyright © 1977, 1979 by The University of the South; *The Collected Poems of Tennessee Williams*, copyright © 1925, 1926, 1932, 1933, 1935, 1936, 1938, 1942, 1944, 1947, 1948, 1949, 1950, 1952, 1956, 1960, 1961, 1963, 1964, 1971, 1975, 1977, 1978, 1979, 1981, 1982, 1983, 1991, 1995, 2002 by The University of the South; *The Collected Stories of Tennessee Williams*, copyright © 1948 by The University of the South, renewed 1976 The University of the South; *The Selected Letters of Tennessee Williams: Volume I, 1920–1945*, edited by Albert J. Devlin and Nancy M. Tischler, copyright © 2000 by The University of the South.

PHOTO CREDITS

FRONTISPIECE.

Tennessee Williams. Photo by Angus McBean, London. Courtesy of New Directions.

PAGE 2.

St. Paul's Episcopal Church. Humanities Research Center. University of Texas at Austin.

PAGE 3.

Thomas Lanier Williams III. Collection of Richard Freeman Leavitt/University of Tennessee.

PAGE 4.

Church Hill chapel. Courtesy of Thomas H. and Joan W. Gandy.

Port Gibson Presbyterian Church. The Mississippi Valley Collection. University of Memphis.

PAGE 5.

Dakin family. Humanities Research Center. University of Texas at Austin.

Edwina Dakin. Humanities Research Center. University of Texas at Austin.

PAGE **6.**

Thomas Lanier Williams II. Humanities Research Center. University of Texas at Austin.

Isabella Coffin Williams. Humanities Research Center. University of Texas at Austin.

Sidney Lanier. Middle Georgia Archives. Washington Memorial Library, Macon, Georgia.

Polly McClung. Courtesy of the McClung Museum, University of Tennessee in Knoxville.

PAGE **7.**

John "Nollichucky Jack" Sevier. Special Collections. University of Tennessee in Knoxville.

Old Gray Cemetery. The History of Homes and Gardens of Tennessee. Courtesy of the McClung Historical Collection. University of Tennessee in Knoxville.

PAGE **9.**

Ella Williams. Collection of Richard Freeman Leavitt/University of Tennessee.

Will and Belle Brownlow. Courtesy of Dakin Williams.

PAGE **10.**

St. Paul's Rectory. Harvard Theatre Collection

PAGE **11.**

Cornelius Coffin Williams. Humanities Research Center. University of Texas at Austin.

PAGE **12.**

Tennessee and Douglas Bateman. Courtesy of Mrs. Douglas Bateman.

PAGE **13.**

Tom, age twelve. Humanities Research Center. University of Texas at Austin.

Rose, age seven. Humanities Research Center. University of Texas at Austin.

PAGE **14.**

Production scene, *The Night of the Iguana*. Collection of Richard Freeman Leavitt/University of Tennessee.

PAGE **15.**

The University of the South. Courtesy of University of the South, Sewanee, Tennessee.

Grandmother Rosina Dakin. Courtesy of Dakin Williams.

Grandfather Dakin. Special Collections, Nashville Public Library.

PAGE **16.**

Production still, *Sweet Bird of Youth*. Courtesy of Jack Oatman, Clarksdale, Mississippi.

PAGE **17.**

Buena Vista Hotel. Mississippi Valley Collection. University of Memphis.

PAGE **18.**

Production still, *The Rose Tattoo*. Humanities Research Center. University of Texas at Austin.

PAGE **19.**

John Sharp Williams. Collection of Kenneth Holditch.

PAGE **20.**

Tom, Ozzie, and Rose. Humanities Research Center. University of Texas at Austin.

PAGE **22.**

Rose, Edwina, and Tom. Humanities Research Center. University of Texas at Austin.

PAGE **23.**

Production still, *Cat on a Hot Tin Roof*. Photo by Joseph Abeles. Collection of Richard Freeman Leavitt/University of Tennessee.

PAGE **24.**

Peabody Hotel lobby. Mississippi Valley Collection. University of Memphis.

Catfish Row. Mississippi Valley Collection. University of Memphis.

PAGE **26.**

Mississippi Delta scene. Special Collections, Ekstrom Library, University of Louisville, Kentucky.

PAGE **27.**

Jordan Massee and son. Courtesy of Jordan Massee, Jr.

Burl Ives. Photo by Joseph Abeles. Collection of Richard Freeman Leavitt/University of Tennessee.

PAGE **56.**

Mardi Gras parade. Photo by Arthur Tong. The Historic New Orleans Collection. Collection of Kenneth Holditch.

PAGE **58.**

Rose Williams. Collection of Richard Freeman Leavitt/University of Tennessee.

PAGE **59.**

Lyle Saxon. Rodolph Fuchs Collection, Tammy G. Henry Research Center, Eugene P. Watson Library, Northwestern University of Louisiana.

PAGE **60.**

722 Toulouse Street. Historic New Orleans Collection.

Eloi Bordelon. Abbé and Charles Ayala.

PAGE **63.**

Production still, *Vieux Carré*. Humanities Research Center. University of Texas at Austin.

PAGE **65.**

Tennessee Williams and Jim Parrott. Humanities Research Center. University of Texas at Austin.

PAGE **66.**

Tennessee Williams. Copyright © Christopher R. Harris.

PAGE **68.**

The French Market and Morning Call. Leonard V. Huber, "New Orleans."

PAGE **70.**

Tennessee and Marion Black Vaccaro. Collection of Richard Freeman Leavitt/University of Tennessee.

PAGE **71.**

Tennessee and Tallulah Bankhead. Collection of Richard Freeman Leavitt/University of Tennessee.

PAGE **72.**

Tennessee and Carson McCullers. *Theatre Arts Magazine.*

PAGE **74.**

538 Royal Street. Collection of Kenneth Holditch. Exchange Alley. Jack Beech.

PAGE **75.**

Tennessee, Irene Selzneck, and Oliver Evans. Collection of Richard Freeman Leavitt/University of Tennessee.

PAGE **76.**

The Starlite Lounge. Collection of Kenneth Holditch.

Ruthie the Duck Girl. Courtesy of Marda Burton.

PAGE **78.**

710 Orleans Avenue. Humanities Research Center. University of Texas at Austin.

St. Louis Cathedral. Leonard V. Huber, "New Orleans."

PAGE **79.**

Tennessee Williams. Humanities Research Center. University of Texas at Austin.

PAGE **80.**

Tennessee and Pancho Rodriguez. Collection of Richard Freeman Leavitt/University of Tennessee.

632 St. Peter Street. Photo by Johnny Donnels. Collection of Richard Freeman Leavitt/University of Tennessee.

PAGE **81.**

Jessica Tandy, as Blanche DuBois. Courtesy of Hume Cronyn.

PAGE **82.**

The streetcar named Desire 1949. Photo by Mike Bernadas, New Orleans. Collection of Collection of Richard Freeman Leavitt/University of Tennessee.

PAGE **83.**

Movie still, *A Streetcar Named Desire.* Humanities Research Center. University of Texas at Austin.

PAGE **84.**

Victor's Café. Jack Beech. Collection of Kenneth Holditch.

PAGE **85.**

Tennessee and Grandfather. Mississippi Valley Collection. University of Memphis.

PAGE 86.

Marion Black Vaccaro. Collection of Richard Freeman Leavitt/University of Tennessee.

Tennessee and Frank Merlo. Collection of Richard Freeman Leavitt/University of Tennessee.

PAGE 87.

Maison de Ville. Collection of Kenneth Holditch.

PAGE 88.

Kenneth Holditch and Kim Hunter. Photo by Earl Perry. Collection of Kenneth Holditch.

PAGE 89.

1014 Dumaine Street. Collection of Kenneth Holditch.

PAGE 90.

Tennessee Williams in Marti's Restaurant. Photo by Sam Shaw. Collection of Richard Freeman Leavitt/University of Tennessee.

Lafitte's Blacksmith Shop. Collection of Kenneth Holditch.

PAGE 91.

Tennessee in The Court of Sisters. Copyright © Christopher R. Harris.

PAGE 92.

Tennessee in Jackson Square. Copyright © Christopher R. Harris.

Tennessee and the Preservation Hall band. Copyright © Christopher R. Harris.

PAGE 93.

Tennessee and the cast of *One Mo' Time*. Photo by David Richmond, New Orleans.

PAGE 94.

Tennessee and Lyle Leverich. Photo by David Richmond, New Orleans.

PAGE 95.

Tennessee Williams. Wright Langley, Key West.

PAGE 96.

Tennessee Williams. Photo by Jan Deen. Collection of Richard Freeman Leavitt/University of Tennessee.

PAGE 97.

Tennessee beside St. Louis Cathedral. Copyright © Christopher R. Harris.

PAGE 98.

Tennessee's gravestone. Courtesy of Allean Hale.

Crowd outside the Hotel Elysée. Collection of Richard Freeman Leavitt/University of Tennessee.

Entrance to Calvary Cemetery. Collection of Richard Freeman Leavitt/University of Tennessee.

PAGE 99.

Wreath on door. Collection of Ed Boardman.

PAGE 100.

Draped streetcar. Collection of Edward Boardman.

PAGE 101.

New Orleans memorial service. Photo by David Richmond, New Orleans.

PAGE 105.

Tennessee Williams. Collection of Richard Freeman Leavitt/University of Tennessee.